STUDENT SOLUTIONS TO ACCOMPANY

FINANCIAL

Accounting

A User Perspective

Third Canadian Edition

Robert E. Hoskin
University of Connecticut

Maureen R. Fizzell
Simon Fraser University

JOHN WILEY & SONS CANADA, LTD

National Library of Canada Cataloguing in Publication

Hoskin, Robert E., 1949-
    Student solutions manual to accompany Financial accounting: a user perspective, third Canadian edition / Robert E. Hoskin, Maureen R. Fizzell.

ISBN 0-470-83403-X

    1. Accounting—Study and teaching (Higher) 2. Accounting—Problems, exercises, etc. I. Fizzell, Maureen II. Hoskin, Robert E., 1949-   . Accounting. III. Title.

HF5635.H68 2003 Suppl. 2   657'.044   C2003-903946-3

Production Credits

Publisher: John Horne
Publishing Services Director: Karen Bryan
Editorial Manager: Karen Staudinger
Marketing Manager: Carolyn J. Wells
Printing and Binding: Tri-Graphic Printing Limited

Printed and bound in Canada
10 9 8 7 6 5 4 3 2 1

John Wiley & Sons Canada Ltd
22 Worcester Road
Etobicoke, Ontario
M9W 1L1
Visit our website at: www.wiley.ca

CHAPTER 1

Overview of Corporate Financial Reporting

ASSESSING YOUR RECALL SOLUTIONS

1-1   A private corporation is one whose ownership shares are held by a small number of individuals. This makes the transfer of ownership more difficult as the shares do not trade on a public stock exchange. A public corporation has shares held by a larger number of individuals or entities and these shares are bought and sold on a public stock exchange (such as the Toronto Stock Exchange).

1-3   Three types of information that users should be able to learn from financial statements are:

1. management's ability to profitably manage the company
2. the company's investment in assets
3. the company's ability to repay debt
4. the company's compliance with regulations
5. the financial health of the company

(Note: This list could be expanded to include other types of information.)

1-5   The major qualitative characteristics that accounting information should possess are:

Understandability – The information must be understandable to a reasonably well-informed user.

Relevance – The information must be relevant for the decision under consideration. Relevance consists of several sub-characteristics:

> *Timeliness* – The information must be received on a timely basis in order to make a difference in decision-making.
>
> *Predictive Value and/or Feedback Value* – In order to be useful, the information must provide the user with the ability to predict some future outcome or to evaluate a past decision.

Reliability – The information must be reliable to be of use to a decision maker. Reliability has four sub-characteristics:

> *Verifiability* – The information must be capable of being verified or reproduced by the user.
>
> *Neutrality* – The information must not be produced in a biased way relative to the effects it has on the entity being measured.
>
> *Representational Faithfulness* – The information must represent what it purports to represent.
>
> *Conservatism* – Any estimates that are made in the financial statements should err on the side of understating net assets and net income rather than overstating them.

Comparability – Information produced by different companies must be understood by users so that they can make comparisons across companies. Companies are not required to use the same accounting methods. Therefore, users must understand the impact of the various methods allowed under GAAP.

1-7 The three major categories of items that appear in a typical balance sheet are assets, liabilities, and shareholders' equity.

Assets are those things that a company owns or has the right to use and which have probable future value. The company is able to perform its activities and thereby generate profits with the help of its assets, which means that they are income earning. Assets may be current or non-current. Current assets will be converted into cash within the next year or operating cycle. Examples include cash, inventory, and accounts receivable. Non-current assets are those assets whose benefits may be realized over a period longer than one year or operating cycle. Examples include property, plant, and equipment, patents, trademarks, etc.

Liabilities are the amounts that the company owes to others and which require a probable future sacrifice of resources. Liabilities may be classified as current and non-current. Current liabilities include notes payable due within one year, accounts payable, accrued expenses, and dividends payable. Non-current liabilities include long-term debt, long-term warranties payable, and pension liabilities.

Shareholders' Equity represents the wealth or the ownership interest of the owners. Shareholders' equity may also be defined as the difference between the assets and liabilities of a company:

Shareholders' Equity = Assets – Liabilities

There are two major shareholders' equity accounts: share capital and retained earnings. Share capital represents the amount that investors originally paid for the share that the company issued. Retained earnings consist of the earnings of the company less the dividends paid.

1-9 The notes to the financial statements provide more detail about items in the financial statements and are cross-referenced. The first or second note to the financial statements often discusses the Summary of Accounting Policies, which describes the choices made by management from among the possible choices and judgements acceptable under GAAP.

APPLYING YOUR KNOWLEDGE SOLUTIONS

1-11 a) The business experiences of Raj Randhawa illustrate that accounting is similar to a scorecard, because, like a scorecard that keeps track of past events, accounting keeps track of past transactions. This enables users to measure the company's performance. For example, Mr. Randhawa describes how he regularly checks the accounting system to receive feedback on past decisions and receive input for his next business strategy.

Just as a scorecard keeps track of the score in a tennis game, companies need a system to keep track of their historical transactions. Accounting is this "scorecard system" that provides users with decision-making information. And while accounting is more complex than a simple scorecard, practitioners have developed Generally Accepted Accounting Principles (GAAP), which companies are required to follow in order to provide users with timely, reliable, and relevant information. Thus, accounting and a scorecard have a lot in common. Think about your own experience using a scorecard to record a past event, like a golf game, and you will notice a lot of similarity between the two. Both keep track of historical events in a fair and objective way, and give users feedback on their performance.

b) Mr. Randhawa decided to focus "more on service— programming, network support, and so on—than on hardware sales" in order to improve the company's profit margins. He also decided to obtain a bank loan to finance renovations and improvements, rather than relying on a line of credit.

1-13 Examples of Bombardier's financing transactions:
1. Share issuance to raise capital for acquisition of manufacturing equipment
2. Increase in long-term debt to raise capital

Examples of Bombardier's investing transactions:
1. Purchase of manufacturing equipment
2. Sale of plant (land and buildings)

Examples of Bombardier's operating transactions:

1. Sale of skidoos (a Bombardier Inc. product line)
2. Payment of wages payable

1-15 This information would suggest that Matrix Technologies may face reduced sales revenues and net income in the future. Also, the collectibility of any amount owing to Matrix from the customer may be in doubt. Readers of the quarterly report would likely find such information relevant as it would help in predicting reduced levels of future income and cash flow. Providing the information now about an expected future decline in sales provides more timely information to users of the quarterly report, and thus, enables them to make earlier and better informed investment decisions.

1-17 a) CA
b) CL
c) IS
d) CA
e) RE and/or SCF
f) IS
g) NCA
h) SC and/or SCF
i) CA and/or SCF
j) NCL

1-19 a) NCA
b) IS
c) SCF
d) NCL
e) RE
f) IS
g) CL
h) SCF
i) CA
j) NCA

1-21 a) FA
      b) OA
      c) IA
      d) FA
      e) OA
      f) FA
      g) IA
      h) FA

1-23 a) BS
      b) IS
      c) BS
      d) BS
      e) N (Balance sheet shows ending balance of PP&E, not purchases in period)
      f) IS
      g) IS
      h) BS
      i) N (Balance sheet shows bank loan balance at a point in time, not amount secured)
      j) BS

1-25

	A	B	C	D
Current Assets	$ 600,000	**$300,000**	$120,000	$ 420,000
Non-current Assets	**900,000**	650,000	**350,000**	750,000
Total Assets	1,500,000	**950,000**	470,000	**1,170,000**
Current Liabilities	400,000	300,000	80,000	200,000
Non-current Liabilities	350,000	**250,000**	190,000	**370,000**
Shareholders' Equity	**750,000**	400,000	**200,000**	600,000
Total Liabilities and Shareholders' Equity	**1,500,000**	950,000	**470,000**	**1,170,000**

1-27 a)

Bouquet Scents Ltd.
Income Statement
for the month of July, 2xxx

Sales		$24,730
Cost of flowers	$10,733	
Employee wages	7,000	
Rent	1,500	
Electricity and water	370	
Gas and repairs	329	
Telephone	160	
Total Expenses		20,092
Net Income		$ 4,638

b) Other costs that Jackson might have incurred in July not listed above include:

1. Amortization of delivery vehicle

2. GST and corporate taxes

3. Interest paid on any outstanding loans

1-29 a)

Item	Classification
Inventory	Asset
Wages owed	Liability
Bank loan	Liability
Cash held in bank	Asset
Cost of refrigerators	Asset
Prepaid rent	Asset
Common shares	Shareholders' equity
Retained Earnings	Shareholders' equity

b)

Bouquet Scents Ltd.
Balance Sheet
July 31, 2xxx

Cash	$ 8,361	Wages owed	$ 950
Inventory	1,100	Bank loan	8,000
Prepaid rent	1,500		
		Common Shares	18,000
Refrigerators	18,695	Retained Earnings	2,706
Total Assets	$ 29,656	Total Shareholders' Equity and Liabilities	$29,656

c) It is unlikely that Jackson will have an account called 'accounts receivable' since most of his sales will be on a cash basis. If customers purchased flowers on credit, then Jackson would have an accounts receivable section on his balance sheet that would represent the amount that he is owed from his customers. However, florists sell products that are relatively cheap, therefore most customers, if not all, will have enough funds to pay for their purchase in their wallet, which is why it is unlikely that Jackson will have an account called 'accounts receivable.' The exception might be if Jackson has a standing order to deliver flowers to a customer (such as a hotel) on a weekly basis. In this case, the cost of the order may be large, and the customer is probably long-standing and well trusted, so that Jackson would feel comfortable extending credit to the hotel in this situation.

1-31 *Suncor Energy Inc.*
Assets
- Oil and gas reserves
- Exploration equipment
Liabilities
- Long-term debt

Ballard Power Systems Inc.
Assets
- Equipment for research
- Accounts receivable
Liabilities
- Wages payable

Danier Leather Inc.
Assets
- Inventory (clothing for sale)
- Receivables from customers
- Manufacturing equipment (sewing machines)
Liabilities
- Long-term debt
- Accounts Payable

Quebecor Inc.
Assets
- Equipment (printing presses)
- Newsprint supplies
- Accounts receivable

Liabilities
- Wages payable
- Long-term debt

Bombardier Inc.
Assets
- Construction in process
- Inventory for sale
- Manufacturing equipment
Liabilities
- Interest payable
- Wages payable

Royal Bank
Assets
- Securities investments
- Cash
- Mortgage loans receivable

Liabilities
- Customer deposits

Westjet Airlines Ltd.
Assets
- Aircraft
- Prepaid rent (landing rights)
- Fuel inventory

Liabilities
- Prepaid tickets

1-33 *Suncor Energy Inc.*
Statement of Cash Flows
- Investment in gas properties
- Purchase of drilling equipment

Ballard Power Systems Inc.
Statement of Cash Flows
- Investment in equipment
- Investment in research and development

Danier Leather Inc.
Statement of Cash Flows
- Increase/decrease in inventory
- Purchase of manufacturing equipment

Quebecor Inc.
Statement of Cash Flows
- Repayment of bank loans
- Cash proceeds from sale of printing equipment

Bombardier Inc.
Statement of Cash Flows
- Debt issuance
- Common shares issued
- Purchase of manufacturing equipment

Royal Bank
Statement of Cash Flows

- Purchase of securities
- Increase/decrease in customer deposits

Westjet Airlines Ltd.
Statement of Cash Flows
- Cash proceeds from sale of aircraft
- Increase/decrease in fuel inventories

USER PERSPECTIVE SOLUTIONS

1-35 As noted in the answer to 1-34, in deciding whether to purchase the vehicles, the controller should:

Assess the company's cash position:
- Interest lost on cash balances, if no borrowing required
- Ability to borrow from the bank, and interest rate (if the company must borrow the purchase price)

Determine the long-term desirability of owning the vehicles:
- Will newer, more efficient models become available?
- What is the second hand market for the vehicle if the company later decides to sell?

1-37 Accounting for inventory at its current market price rather than at its historical cost would be more relevant for users in that it would help them to better predict the future cash flows generated from the sale of that inventory (predictive value). At the same time, accounting for inventory at its current market price would be less reliable, because market value tends to fluctuate, and is thus less verifiable than historical cost. Due to the potential uncertainty in determining market value, the principle of conservatism also applies, suggesting the use of historical cost.

1-39 a) A bank loan officer would request that financial statements be prepared according to GAAP because GAAP has established guidelines for the preparation of financial statements that would provide some assurance to the loan officer that the reporting followed some basic format. Furthermore, statements prepared according to GAAP are intended to satisfy qualitative criteria such as relevance, reliability, understandability, and comparability.

b) You could convince the loan officer that the statements were prepared according to GAAP through appointing an auditor to express an opinion on the financial statements.

c) The loan officer would be interested in your company's ability to repay the loan and thus would look at net income and cash flows. The loan officer would also need to consider a backup plan in the event your company does not make the required loan payments. For example, which assets of your company could be given to the bank in lieu of repayment, or sold to provide cash for repayment? The loan officer would also look at your balance sheet to identify the assets owned by your company, but would prefer up-to-date market values for these assets rather than the purchase costs listed on the balance sheet.

1-41 Funds can be raised from several sources, but the two primary sources are from lenders and shareholders. The advantage of borrowing from a lender is that your friend would retain complete ownership of the business and would not be required to share the decision-making and the profit of the company with anyone else. Bringing in another shareholder would obviously result in a loss of control over the company and would also mean giving up some share of the future profits. The disadvantage of borrowing from a lender is that the loan contracts will require repayment of the amount on a set schedule. This increases the risk to the company that it will not be able to make payments on a timely basis. There could be significant consequences to not making payments, including losing ownership of the business. A new shareholder would not have this same type of contractual arrangement and would be at risk in the same way as your friend. However, the new shareholder would probably expect a higher return from her/his investment than would a lender. Therefore, your friend would be giving up more potential profit to a new shareholder than a lender. There are also tax incentives for borrowing in that, from a corporate point of view, the interest payments on a loan are deductible for tax purposes. Payments to shareholders (such as dividends) are not tax deductible.

1-43 The board should consider the number of shares outstanding and the proposed dividend per share, which will determine the total cash requirements. They must also consider whether the available cash in the business is sufficient to make the dividend payment. If not, they may have to delay payment of the dividend (it can still be declared), or look for ways to generate additional cash.

The dividend declaration will reduce retained earnings, so the retained earnings amount should be larger than the proposed dividend. The board should also consider the company's future plans. The retained earnings account represents the cumulative profit of the business that is kept within the company to fund future expansion plans. Dividends are declared and paid when the company has no plans to use the profit to fund future expansion. Thus, the declaration and payment of the dividend only makes sense if the company does not need the cash for future expansion plans.

READING AND INTERPRETING PUBLISHED FINANCIAL STATEMENTS SOLUTIONS

1-45 Figures from the Consolidated Balance Sheet (all amounts in millions):

Total Assets	=	Total Liabilities + Shareholders' Equity
$3,880	=	$2,260.1 + $1,619.9
$3,880	=	$3,880

1-47 Largest sources of cash (in millions of dollars):

Cash generated by operating activities	$241.7
Issue of long-term obligations	$200.0

Largest uses of cash (in millions of dollars):

Purchases of capital assets	($143.4)
Repayment of long-term obligations	($110.6)

1-49 Total revenues in 2001 were $370.6 million higher than in 2000, yet net income declined $131.7 million to $94.1 million. The reason is that cost of merchandise sold, operating, administrative, and selling expenses increased proportionately more than revenues. These costs increased by $482.0 million in the last year. As a result, while Sears Canada had $517.8 of earnings in 2000 after covering these costs, the margin dropped to only $405.5 million in 2001. Also, 2001 depreciation and amortization expenses were higher by $39.5 million than in 2000, which further decreased 2001 net income.

1-51 Figures from the Consolidated Balance Sheet (in thousands):

Total Assets	=	Total Liabilities + Shareholders' Equity
$4,371,156	=	$1,993,133 + $2,378,023
$4,371,156	=	$4,371,156

1-53 (All amounts in thousands)

    a) $5,374,759
    b) $5,097,783
    c) $88,036
    d) $99,712
    e) $176,653
    f) $440,935
    g) $1,038,471
    h) $973,050
    i) $1,115,027
    j) $186,943
    k) $358,229
    l) $225,000
    m) $468,833

1-55 Largest sources of cash (in thousands of dollars):

1. Cash generated by operations	$361,642
2. Proceeds on sale of limited partnerships	$300,000

Largest uses of cash (in thousands of dollars):

1. Additions to property and equipment	($358,229)
2. Investment in credit charge receivables	($317,597)

1-57 At $42.00/share, total market value = $143,781,372
At $30.50/share, total market value = $104,412,663

Average market value = $124,097,018

Balance sheet value of shareholders' equity at end of 2001, $1,603,694.

The Statement of Earnings and Retained Earnings indicate that there was a weighted average number of $78,652,610 common and Class A Non-Voting shares outstanding at the end of 2001. So the common shareholders share the value of the company with the Class A shareholders. Thus the market value of the common shares is less than the total value of the company as indicated on the balance sheet—that is, the balance sheet value of $1,603,694 also includes the value of the company attributable to the Class A shareholders.

1-59 (All amounts in thousands)
   a) $81,640
   b) $31,428
   c) $1,286
   d) $3,708
   e) $7,002
   f) $6,144
   g) $10,836
   h) $24,552
   i) $5,553
   j) $319
   k) $(12,057)
   l) $(150)
   m) $5,395
   n) $(5,841)

1-61 Largest sources of cash (in thousands of dollars):

   1. Proceeds on maturity/disposal of short-term
      marketable securities $31,305
   2. Issue of common shares and warrants $5,395

   Largest uses of cash (in thousands of dollars):

   1. Acquisition of short-term marketable securities $(19,674)
   2. Acquisition of capital assets—net $(12,057)

1-63 Assets: Increase in accounts receivable $13,626
                    Decrease in short-term marketable
                       securities $11,631
                    Increase in long-term investments $5,415

Liabilites: Increase in accounts payable and
accrued liabilities $3,061
Decrease in deferred revenue $588
Decrease in mortgage payable $13

1-65 METRO INC.'s fiscal year end is the last Saturday in September each year.

1-67

Total liabilities	$628	53%
Total shareholders' equity	558	47
(in millions)	$1,186	100%

The company is financed primarily by creditors (53% of total assets), although the financing from shareholders is of a roughly similar level.

1-69 (All amounts in millions)
In the year 2001, retained earnings:

Increased by:
- $122.8 due to net earnings

Decreased by:
- $17.3 due to dividends declared and paid
- $5.4 due to share redemption premium (company bought back its own shares and paid more to buy them back than the shares were originally issued for)
- $6.0 due to stock options settled in cash

1-71 The company's fiscal year end is December 31.

1-73

Total liabilities	156,865	78.7%
Total shareholders' equity	42,409	21.3
	199,274	100%

The business is financed primarily by creditors (78.7% of total assets). The proportion was roughly similar in 1999 (79.4%).

BEYOND THE BOOK SOLUTIONS

1-75 No answer required.

1-77 Answers to this question will depend on the company selected.

CHAPTER 2

Transaction Analysis and Accounting Entries

ASSESSING YOUR RECALL SOLUTIONS

2-1   When transactions are recorded in the accounting system, the equality of the basic accounting equation, Assets = Liabilities + Shareholders' Equity, must be maintained. This implies that all transactions must affect at least two accounts in the financial statements to maintain the equality, although the effects may be within the same category of accounts. For example, the collection of cash from customers on account both increases an asset (cash) and decreases another asset (accounts receivable).

2-3   Advantages of using the cash basis:

1. Revenue is recognized when cash is received. Under the accrual system, some of the revenues are recognized before the cash is received. The uncertainty of the future cash flow is captured by estimates of potential uncollectibility. Indeed, under the accrual system some of the revenues may never be received at all.
2. It is beneficial to businesses with small investments where cash is realized soon after the services are rendered.
3. It is a simple method of accounting in terms of the number of accounting entries involved.

Disadvantages of using the cash basis:

1. Expenses incurred in generating revenues may not be matched in the same period.

2. Revenues may not reflect the sales effort for the period because credit sales would not be recorded until the cash is received.

3. The cash basis does not give a fair view of the profit/loss for the fiscal year because some sales are missed and some expenses are missed because they have not yet been paid for.

2-5 a) T
b) F
c) F
d) F
e) T
f) F
g) F
h) T

2-7 Under GAAP, revenues are recognized on the accrual basis, where the recording of revenues (and expenses) is in the period in which they are earned (incurred) rather than when the cash event occurs. Revenue recognition criteria are criteria used to determine when revenues should be recognized from a sales transaction. The amount recognized must be reasonable and there must also be a high probability that cash will ultimately be collected. The matching concept requires that all expenses associated with the generation of revenues should be matched with the respective revenues.

2-9 Under accrual-basis accounting, an accrued expense is one that is recognized on the income statement as an expense before cash is paid out. In this case, a liability is set up on the balance sheet that will be eliminated once the cash has been paid.

2-11 Amortization is a method of allocating the cost of a non-current asset to each of the years of its useful life. Using the straight-line method, amortization is calculated as the total cost of the asset less the estimated residual value divided by the estimated number of years of useful life.

APPLYING YOUR KNOWLEDGE SOLUTIONS

2-13 Cash Basis:

Cash sales	$105,000
Cash collections on credit sales	34,000
Less:	
Payments to suppliers	75,500
Wages paid	23,000
Insurance premiums paid	900
INCOME	$ 39,600

Accrual Basis:

Cash sales	$105,000
Credit sales	36,000
Less:	
Cost of Goods Sold	79,000
Wages expense	23,900
Insurance expense	225
INCOME	$ 37,875

2-15 A balance in retained earnings means that the business has been profitable in the past and the profits have been retained within the company. It does not mean that the profits are in the form of cash. More than likely the profits have been invested in other assets such as property, plant, and equipment and inventory. To the extent that these assets can be sold for their carrying values, the statement is somewhat correct—the proceeds could be used to pay off liabilities. If the assets are not worth their carrying values or they are difficult to turn into cash (such as investments in real estate), the statement is not entirely correct. Retained earnings do provide some level of comfort during difficult times as their existence means that assets exceed liabilities.

2-17

Account	Increase/Decrease
a. A – Cash	Increase
SE – Common Shares	Increase
b. A – Equipment	Increase
L – Accounts Payable	Increase
c. A – Inventory	Increase
A – Cash	Decrease
L – Accounts Payable	Increase
d. A – Accounts Receivable	Increase
SE – Sales Revenue	Increase*
SE – Cost of Goods Sold	Increase**
A – Inventory	Decrease
e. A – Cash	Increase
A – Accounts Receivable	Decrease
f. A – Cash	Increase
L – Loan Payable	Increase
g. SE – Dividends Declared	Increase**
L – Dividend Payable	Increase
h. L – Dividends Payable	Decrease
A – Cash	Decrease
i. SE – Wage Expenses	Increase**
L - Accrued Wages	Increase
j. A – Office supplies	Increase
A – Cash	Decrease

* Increase in Shareholders' Equity
** Decrease in Shareholders' Equity

2-19

	Income	Cash Flow
a.	No Effect	+$60,000
b.	+$245	No effect (sold on account, inventory already owned)
c.	No Effect	-$1,200
d.	-$500	No Effect
e.	No Effect	No Effect
f.	No Effect	-$950
g.	No Effect	+$100
h.	No Effect	No Effect
i.	No Effect	-$2,000

2-21   **Assets = Liabilities + Shareholders' Equity**

a) +15,000 (supplies)   = +15,000 (accounts payable)
b) +25,000 (cash)   = +25,000 [retained earnings
                                        (service revenue)]
   -8,000 (supplies) = -8,000 [retained earnings
                                        (cost of sales)]
c) +25,000 (cash)   = +25,000 (common shares)
d)   = +500 (warranty payable)
                          -500 [retained earnings
                                        (warranty expense)]
e) -14,000 (cash)   = -14,000 (accounts payable)
f) -575 (cash)   = +75 (accounts payable)
                          -650 [retained earnings
                                        (utility expense)]
g) +50,000 (cash)   = +50,000 (bank loan)
h) +48,000 (equipment)= -48,000 (cash)
i) -7,000 (cash)   = -7,000 [retained earnings
                                        (wages expense)]

2-23

	Assets	=	**Liabilities**	+	**Shareholders' Equity**
a.	+$12,500 (cash)	=	+$12,500 (bank loan)		
b.	-$1,000 (cash)	=		+	-$1,000 [retained earnings (interest expense)]
c.	+$8,000 (equipment) -$8,000 (cash)				
d.	-$1,200 (equipment)	=		+	-$1,200 [retained earnings (amortization expense)]

e. +$35,500
[cash of
$28,000 +
accounts
receivable of
$7,500]
-$21,600
(inventory)

= + +$13,900 [sales of
$35,500 less cost of
goods sold expense of
$21,600)]

f. +$6,800
(cash)
-$6,800
(accounts
receivable)

g. +$24,700
(inventory)
= +$24,700
(accounts
payable)

h. -$22,900
(cash)
= -$22,900
(accounts
payable)

i. = +2,400
(salaries
payable)
+ -$2,400 [retained earnings
(wages expense)]

j. -$2,350 (cash) = -$2,350
(salaries
payable
+

k. -$400 (cash) = + -$400 (retained earnings)

2-25

	Assets	=	Liabilities	+	Shareholders' Equity
1/1/04	$150,000	=	$85,000	+	$65,000

a. +$40,000 (land)
    -$40,000 (cash)

b. +$20,000   = +$20,000 (note
    (equipment)   payable)

c. -$27,000 (cash)   = -$27,000

d. +$50,000 (cash)   =   + +$50,000 (common
                                           shares)

e. +$10,000 (cash)   = +$10,000 (note
                            payable)

TOTAL **$203,000**   = **$88,000**   + **$115,000**

2-27

a)

Sara's Bakery
Income Statement
For the year ended December 31, 20x1

Sales	$95,000
Cost of goods sold	52,000
Gross Profit	$43,000

Less operating expenses:		
Wage expense	$22,000	
Rent expense	9,600	
Total expenses		31,600
Net Income		$ 11,400

b) We did not use the following items on the income statement:

1. **Cash** – This is an asset and belongs on the balance sheet. It is measured at a point in time.

2. **Accounts payable** – This liability item represents an obligation that Sara's Bakery has to its

suppliers/creditors. It is also measured at a point in time and belongs on the balance sheet.

3. **Common shares** – This is a component of shareholders' equity on the balance sheet. It represents the amount of capital contributed to the business in exchange for an ownership interest. It does not measure performance of the company's operations, and thus, does not belong on the income statement.

2-29

a)

The Garment Tree Ltd.
Income Statement
For the year ended December 31, 20x1

Sales		$120,000
Cost of goods sold		52,000
Gross Profit		$ 68,000
Less expenses:		
Wage expense	$32,000	
Rent expense	9,600	
Advertising expense	5,000	
Miscellaneous expense	5,000	
Total expenses		51,600

b) We did not use the following items on the income statement:

1. **Wages payable** – This liability item reflects the wages owed by The Garment Tree Ltd. to its employees for hours worked but not yet paid. Wage expense, however, already includes the amount of wages payable on the income statement because accrual accounting records an expense in the period that it occurs, not when cash is paid. Wages payable is listed as a liability on the balance sheet.

2. **Inventory** – This asset on the balance sheet is not placed on the income statement because it represents the cost of inventory that is sitting in storage. Once the products are sold to customers, accrual accounting takes the costs of the inventory and records it as cost of goods sold. In the meantime, inventory remains an asset on the balance sheet, representing the cost of products not yet sold.

2-31 a) To identify the income statement accounts and calculate net income, an income statement for Minute Print Company is presented below.

Minute Print Company
Income Statement
For the year ended December 31, 20x1

Sales		$488,000
Less expenses		
Supplies used	$204,000	
Wages	62,000	
Amortization	30,000	
Rent	24,000	
Other expense	9,000	
Total expenses		329,000
Net Income		$159,000

b) Net Income	$159,000
Less dividends declared	3,000
Retained earnings at Dec 31, 20x1	$156,000

c)

Minute Print Company
Balance Sheet
As at December 31, 20x1

ASSETS
Current assets
    Cash $44,000
    Supplies   18,000
    Prepaid rent   2,000
       Total current assets $64,000
Non-current assets
    Equipment   230,000

Total Assets $294,000

LIABILITIES & SHAREHOLDERS' EQUITY
Current liabilities
    Accounts payable $ 8,000
Non-current liabilities
    Bank loan (assumed non-current)   30,000
    Total liabilities $38,000

Shareholders' equity
    Common shares $100,000
    Retained earnings   156,000
    Total shareholders' equity   256,000

Total Liabilities and Shareholders'
    equity $294,000

2-33 a)

	Assets	=	Liabilities	+	Shareholders' Equity
1.	+$175,000 (cash)	=		+	+$175,000 (common shares)

2. +$125,000 (cash) = +$125,000 (bank loan)

3. +$200,000 [land $60,000 and building $140,000] -$200,000 (cash)

4. +$100,000 (inventory) = +$100,000 (accounts payable)

5. +$75,000 (investment) -$75,000 (cash)

6. +$190,000 [$30,000 cash and $160,000 accounts receivable] = + +$190,000 [retained earnings (sales revenue)]

7. +$135,000 (cash) -$135,000 (accounts receivable)

8. -$92,000 (cash) = -$92,000 (accounts payable)

9. -$44,000 (cash) = + -$44,000 [retained earnings (wages expense)]

10. -$90,000 (inventory) = + -$90,000 [retained earnings (cost of goods sold)]

11. -$6,000 (building) = + -$6,000 [retained earnings (amortization expense)]

12.   -$10,312.50 (cash)*   =   +$937.50 (interest payable)   +   -$11,250 [retained earnings (interest expense)]

13.   +$5,000 (cash)   =   +   +$5,000 [retained earnings (investment income)]

14.   =   +$15,000 (dividends payable)   +   -$15,000 (retained earnings)

TOTAL   **$352,687. 50**   =   **$148,937.50**   +   **$203,750**

*$125,000 x .09 x 1/12 = $937.50 per month
For 11 months = $10,312.50

b)

T. George Company
Income Statement
For the Year Ending December 31, 2004

Revenues		
Sales	$190,000	
Investment income	5,000	
		$195,000
Expenses		
Cost of Goods Sold	90,000	
Wages	44,000	
Interest	11,250	
Amortization	6,000	151,250
NET INCOME		$ 43,750

T. George Company
Balance Sheet
as at December 31, 2004

ASSETS	
Cash	$ 48,687.50
Accounts Receivable	25,000.00

Inventory	10,000.00
Investments	75,000.00
Land	60,000.00
Building	134,000.00
TOTAL ASSETS	$352,687.50

LIABILITIES

Accounts Payable	$ 8,000.00
Dividends Payable	15,000.00
Interest Payable	937.50
Bank Loan	125,000.00
TOTAL LIABILITIES	$148,937.50

SHAREHOLDERS' EQUITY

Common Shares	175,000.00
Retained Earnings	28,750.00
TOTAL SHAREHOLDERS' EQUITY	$203,750.00

TOTAL LIABILITIES AND SHAREHOLDERS' EQUITY	$352,687.50

T. George Company
Cash Flow Statement
For the Year Ending December 31, 2004

Cash Flow from Operating Activities:

Cash collections from customers	$165,000.00
Cash payments to suppliers	(92,000.00)
Cash payments for interest	(10,312.50)
Cash payments for salaries	(44,000.00)
Cash from Operations:	$18,687.50

Cash Flow from Investing Activities:

Cash dividends received	$ 5,000.00
Purchase of Land and Building	(200,000.00)
Purchase of Investment in shares	(75,000.00)
Cash from investing	(270,000.00)

Cash Flow from Financing Activities:

Cash proceeds from Issuance of shares	$ 175,000.00
Cash proceeds from bank loan	125,000.00
Cash from financing	300,000.00

TOTAL INCREASE IN CASH $ 48,687.50

2-35

a)

	Assets	=	Liabilities	+	Shareholders' Equity
1.	+$375,000 (cash)	=		+	+$375,000 (common shares)
2.	+$85,000 (land) +$340,000 (building) -$50,000 (cash)			+	+$375,000 (common shares)
3a	+$100,000 (equipment) -$50,000 (cash)	=	+$50,000 (notes payable)		
3b		=	+$2,500 (interest payable)	+	-$2,500* [retained earnings (interest expense)]
4.	-$5,000 (equipment)	=		+	-$5,000** [retained earnings (amortization expense)]
5.	-$10,000 (building)	=		+	-$10,000*** [retained earnings (amortization expense)]

6.   +$200,000 (inventory)   = +$200,000 (accounts payable)

7.   +$40,000 (cash) +$175,000 (accounts receivable)   =   + $215,000 [retained earnings (sales revenue)]

8.   -$160,000 (inventory)   =   + -$160,000 [retained earnings (cost of goods sold)]

9.   -$175,000 (cash)   = -$175,000 (accounts payable)

10.   +$165,000 (cash) -$165,000 (accounts receivable)

11.   +$20,000 (cash)   = +$5,000 (unearned rent)   + +$15,000 [retained earnings (rental revenue)]

12.   -$30,000 (cash)   =   + -$30,000 [retained earnings (S&D expense)]

13.   -$3,000 (cash)   = +$3,750 (taxes payable)   + -$6,750**** [retained earnings (inc. tax exp.)]

14.   -$3,000 (cash)   = +$1,000 (dividends payable)   + -$4,000 (retained earnings)

TOTAL   **$849,000**   = **$87,250**   + **$761,750**

*$50,000 x .10 x 1/2 = $2,500
**$100,000 ÷ 10 x 1/2 = $5,000
***($340,000 − 40,000) ÷ 30 = $10,000

****See income statement for calculation

A.J. Smith Company
Income Statement
For the year ended December 31, 20x1

Sales		$215,000
Rent revenue		15,000
Total revenues		$230,000
Expenses		
Cost of goods sold	$160,000	
Amortization expense	15,000	
Interest expense	2,500	
Selling and administrative	30,000	207,500
Income before income taxes		22,500
Income taxes		6,750
Net income		$15,750

A.J. Smith Company
Balance Sheet
As at December 31, 20x1

Assets	
Cash	$289,000
Accounts receivable	10,000
Inventory	40,000
Land	85,000
Building	330,000
Equipment	95,000
Total assets	$849,000

Liabilities

Accounts payable	$ 25,000
Notes payable	50,000
Interest payable	2,500
Unearned rent	5,000
Income tax payable	3,750
Dividend payable	1,000
Total liabilities	87,250

Shareholders' equity

Common shares	$750,000
Retained earnings	11,750 *
Total shareholders' equity	761,750
Total liabilities and shareholders' equity	$849,000

*Net income – Dividend declared = $15,750 - $4,000 = $11,750

A.J. Smith Company
Cash Flow Statement
For the year ended December 31, 20x1

Operations

Cash receipts from customers	$205,000	
Cash from rent revenue	20,000	
Cash paid for inventory	(175,000)	
Cash paid for selling and administrative expenses	(30,000)	
Cash paid for income taxes	(3,000)	
Cash from operations		$17,000

Finances

Issuance of shares	375,000	
Payment of dividends	(3,000)	
Cash from financing		372,000

Investing

Purchase of capital assets		(100,000)
Increase in cash		$289,000

2-37 a) Buyer: increase assets (inventory) and increase liabilities (accounts payable)

Seller: decrease assets (inventory), increase assets (accounts receivable), increase shareholders' equity (sales), and decrease shareholders' equity (cost of goods sold expense increases)

b) Borrower: increase assets (cash) and increase liabilities (bank loan)

Bank: increase assets (loan receivable) and decrease assets (cash)

c) Company: increase assets (cash) and increase liabilities (unearned revenue)

Customer: decrease assets (cash) and increase assets (prepaid deposit)

d) Company A: increase assets (investment in Company B) and decrease assets (cash)

Company B: increase assets (cash) and increase shareholders' equity (common shares)

e) Company A: increase assets (investment in Company B) and decrease assets (cash)

Company B: no effect because Company B is not a party to the transaction

f) Company: increase assets (prepaid insurance) and decrease assets (cash)

Insurance company: increase assets (cash) and increase liabilities (premiums paid in advance)

USER PERSPECTIVE SOLUTIONS

2-39 Under the cash basis, it is very clear when to recognize revenue and expenses since they are recognized at the time of cash receipt or cash disbursement. Under the accrual basis, management has much more discretion in the recognition of revenues and expenses. The timing of the revenue is determined based on meeting certain revenue recognition criteria that are subject to interpretation and estimation. Expenses are to be matched with revenues, but many expenses are estimated and are therefore somewhat subjective. For example, many computer companies recognize revenue when they ship computers to dealers who can return them. This allows them to recognize revenue very early. The costs of fixing computers under warranties offered to customers must be estimated and expensed when the computers are shipped to dealers (matched to revenues), although the actual costs of warranty claims may not be known for a considerable period of time.

2-41 a) From the perspective of a shareholder of the company, treating the cost of a piece of equipment as an expense at the date of purchase is likely to misstate net income in the current period as well as in future periods. The current period's income is understated because the full cost of the equipment would be deducted in the current period and it would not be matched with the revenue produced from using that equipment since the revenue would come in over a much longer period of time (the useful life of the asset). Future period's income will be overstated since the revenue shown in those periods will not be offset by the expense of using the equipment.

   b) From the perspective of a buyer, the concern would be that no asset would be listed on the balance sheet of the company (since it would already have been expensed). In attempting to value the assets of the company, the buyer would have to recognize that there are some assets that do not appear on the balance sheet, but should be considered in valuing the company.

2-43 a)

Assets:		
Cash		$ 25,000*
Baking Supplies ($40,000 x 20%)		8,000
Ovens		37,000
Liabilities		
Payable on Baking Supplies		$6,000
Payable on Income Taxes Withheld		3,000
Bank Loan Payable ($34,000-10,000)		25,000
*Calculation of cash on hand at end of year:		
Cash Received		
Bank Loan	$ 35,000	
Shareholders' Contribution		
($5,000 x 3)	15,000	
Sale of Products	86,000	$136,000
Cash Paid Out		
Purchase Baking Supplies		
($40,000-$6,000)	$ 34,000	
Rent Payments on		
Cookie Ovens	13,000	
Payment on Bank Loan	10,000	
Payment of Salaries		
($20,000-3,000)	17,000	
Purchase Ovens	37,000	(111,000)
		$ 25,000

b)

Shareholders' Equity	
Total Assets ($25,000 + 8,000 + 37,000)	$ 70,000
Total Liabilities ($6,000 + 3,000 + 25,000)	(34,000)
Total Shareholders' Equity	$ 36,000

c)

The Really Sinful Cookie Shop
Balance Sheet
December 31, 20xx

Cash	$25,000	Payable on baking supplies	$ 6,000
Baking supplies	8,000	Payable on income tax withheld	3,000
Baking ovens	37,000	Bank loan payable	25,000
		Shareholders' equity	36,000
		Total liabilities and	
Total assets	$70,000	shareholders' equity	$70,000

d) The shareholders' proportionate claim on the reported net assets (assets less liabilities) is $3,000 ($36,000 x 25% x 1/3). In light of the profitable operations during the first year, the shareholder should be able to sell his shares for something above $3,000. On the other hand, if he is desperate to get out of the situation, he may be willing to take any amount greater than zero.

READING AND INTERPRETING PUBLISHED FINANCIAL STATEMENTS SOLUTIONS

2-45 (All amount in millions)

a) $25.6 (Consolidated Statement of Retained Earnings)

b)

Accounts receivable, Dec. 30, 2000	$ 942.0
+ Revenue	6,726.4
- Cash collected	- X ??
Accounts receivable, Dec. 29, 2001	$ 871.9

Cash collected = $6,796.5

c)

Inventory, Dec. 30, 2000	$ 1,015.2
+ Purchases	+ X ??
- Cost of goods sold expense	(6,320.9)
Inventory, Dec. 29, 2001	$ 864.5

Purchases = $6,170.2

Accounts payable, Dec. 30, 2000	$ 974.6
+ Purchases	6,170.2
- Cash paid to suppliers	- X ??
Accounts payable, Dec. 29, 2001	$ 769.9

Cash paid to suppliers = $6,374.9

d)

	2001	2000
1. Profit margin ratio	$\dfrac{\$94.1}{\$6,726.4} = 1.40\%$	$\dfrac{\$225.8}{\$6,355.8} = 3.55\%$
2. Return on assets	$\dfrac{\$94.1}{\$3,880.0} = 2.43\%$	$\dfrac{\$225.8}{\$3,955.0} = 5.71\%$
3. Return on equity	$\dfrac{\$94.1}{\$1,619.9} = 5.81\%$	$\dfrac{\$225.8}{\$1,549.3} = 14.57\%$

e) The profitability of the company declined in 2001 from 3.55% of revenues to 1.40%. Revenues had increased 5.83% in 2001 over prior year levels, while costs (costs of merchandise sold, operating, administrative, and selling expenses) had increased 8.27%. As the profit margin ratio of the company was low in 2000 already, the proportionately greater increase in costs over revenues had a significant dampening effect on 2001 profitability ratios.

      The Annual Report discusses adverse market conditions early in 2001 that were made worse due to a lack in consumer confidence following the September 11 terrorist attacks. The company focused on inventory management and reduction of expenses and capital expenditures in 2001. Inventory levels at December 29, 2001 were $150.7 less than the previous year, and despite the actual increase in expenses, operating costs were $180 less than originally budgeted. Thus, the Annual Report acknowledges the weak profitability in 2001 and details the steps the company has undertaken in order to improve profitability in future years.

2-47

a) Big Rock Brewery Ltd. did not declare any dividends in fiscal 2001.

b)

Accounts receivable, Mar. 31, 2000	$1,872,064
+ Revenue	23,199,678
- Cash collected	- X ??
Accounts receivable, Mar. 31, 2001	$1,593,984

Cash collected = $23,477,758

Sales less government tax and commissions should be used since Big Rock did not receive the gross sales proceeds but instead received the net proceeds. Thus the cash collected from customers should be based on the net revenues.

c)

Inventory, Mar. 31, 2000	$2,676,790
+ Purchases	+ X ??
- Cost of goods sold expense	(9,240,503)
Inventory, Mar. 31, 2001	$2,701,982

Purchases = $9,265,695

Accounts payable, Mar. 31, 2000	$1,264,073
+ Purchases	9,265,695
- Cash paid to suppliers	- X ??
Accounts payable, Mar. 31, 2001	$1,393,068

Cash paid to suppliers = $9,136,700

d)

1. Profit Margin = Net Income / Sales after tax and commissions
   2001 Profit margin = $1,352,573 / $23,199,678 = 5.83%

2. Return on assets = Net Income / Average Total Assets
   2001 ROA = $1,352,573 / $30,632,020 = 4.42%

3. Return on equity = Net income / Average Shareholders' Equity
   2001 ROE = $1,352,573 / $17,833,585 = 7.58%

e) Profitability dropped slightly in 2001, by $108,546 (or 7.4%) of the 2000 result. However, despite the drop in profitability, cash provided by operating activities was up significantly, by $975,591, a 40% increase from the prior year. The main reason for the increase in cash from operating activities was the net change in non-cash working capital. The amount was small and had a positive effect on cash flow in 2001 (due primarily to a reduction in accounts receivable), while in the prior year, the net change in non-cash working capital had resulted in a significant outflow of cash.

2-49 (All amounts in thousands)

a) The value of the share capital issued by WestJet Airlines Ltd. in 2001 was $3,878 ($129,268 - $125,390).

b) WestJet Airlines Ltd. did not pay any dividends during fiscal 2001.

c)

Accounts receivable, Dec. 31, 2000	$6,447
+ Revenue	478,393
- Cash collected	- X ??
Accounts receivable, Dec. 31, 2001	$12,211

Cash collected = $472,629

d) From the income statement we notice that amortization expense was $34,332 in 2001. The amount of amortization relating to capital assets would have decreased the carrying value of the capital assets during 2001. Using the balance sheet we notice that capital assets increased by $61,365. This implies that WestJet purchased capital assets in excess of the amortization amount. The statement of cash flows indicates that capital asset additions were $86,789 ($60,518 + $26,271) and disposals of capital assets were $694. Thus the net additions to capital assets were $86,095. The amortization expense of $34,332 would have reduced the capital assets balance, and between these two effects, we would have expected to see capital assets increase during 2001 by $51,763.

e)

1. Profit Margin = Net earnings / Total revenues
    2001 Profit margin = $37,200 / $478,393 = 7.8%

2. Return on assets = Net earnings / Average total assets
    2001 ROA = $37,200 / $365,538 = 10.2%

3. Return on equity = Net earnings / Average shareholders' equity
    2001 ROE = $37,200 / $201,631 = 18.4%

BEYOND THE BOOK SOLUTIONS

2-51 Answers to this question will depend on the company selected.

CHAPTER 3

Double Entry Accounting Systems

ASSESSING YOUR RECALL SOLUTIONS

3-1   Users of financial information rely on this information in decision-making. Users want assurance that the information is complete, accurately recorded, and fairly measures the company's performance. To assist users in understanding financial information, accounting conventions have been developed for recording transactions and preparing financial statements. These allow users to more easily compare information between companies, as different companies are likely to treat similar transactions in a similar manner, meaning that users can more easily understand the information. Financial statements prepared under generally accepted accounting principles (GAAP) assume a basic knowledge of accounting knowledge by the user, which includes an understanding of how transactions are recorded, summarized, and reported.

3-3   **a)** F
b) T
c) F
d) F
e) F
f) T
g) F

3-5   **a)** DR
b) DR
c) DR

d) CR
e) DR
f) CR
g) CR
h) DR
i) DR

3-7 Expense accounts have debit balances, and debit entries increase these accounts. Shareholder's equity accounts normally have credit balances, and debit entries reduce these accounts. These statements are consistent because expenses, which have debit balances, reduce the shareholders' equity account of retained earnings.

3-9 The major sections of the income statement are income from continuing operations (sales of goods and services to customers that are expected to continue in the future), income from non-operating sources (interest income, gain or loss on sale of capital assets, restructuring expenses), income from unusual or infrequent sources (events that do not occur often), provision for income tax (current and future income taxes), income from discontinued operations (business segments that will not continue in the future), and income from extraordinary items (must be unusual, infrequent, and not resulting from management decisions).

3-11 Current items on the balance sheet are those that will be converted into cash (current assets) or require the use of cash (current liabilities) within one year or operating cycle, whichever is longer. Non-current items will not be converted into cash or require the use of cash within one year or operating cycle.

3-13 For discontinued operations, the operating income must be disclosed separately from other income. Separate disclosure of operating income related to discontinued operations flags this portion of income to users of financial statements, helping them to predict future cash flows. The second disclosure is the gain or loss on disposal of the actual business segment.

APPLYING YOUR KNOWLEDGE SOLUTIONS

3-15 a) DR
  b) CR
  c) CR
  d) CR
  e) DR
  f) DR
  g) DR

3-17 a) A-Inventory   3,100
    L-Accounts Payable   3,100

  b) A-Accounts receivable   2,700
    SE-Sales   2,700
    SE-Cost of goods sold   1,800
    A-Inventory   1,800

  c) A-Cash   2,000
    A-Accounts receivable   2,000

  d) A-Cash   12,000
    L-Bank loan   12,000

  e) A-Cash   20,000
    SE-Common shares   20,000

  f)   A-Equipment   7,500
      A-Cash   7,500

3-19 a)   1. A-Cash   200,000
        SE-Common shares   200,000

      2. A-Inventory   460,000
        L-Accounts payable   460,000

3. A-Accounts receivable   650,000
    SE-Sales   650,000
  SE-Cost of goods sold   380,000
    A-Inventory   380,000

4. A-Cash   580,000
    A-Accounts receivable   580,000

5. L-Accounts payable   440,000
    A-Cash   440,000

6. SE-Rent expense   24,000
    A-Cash   24,000

7. SE-Other expenses   24,000
    A-Cash   24,000

8. SE-Wages expense   46,000
    A-Cash   46,000

9. A-Vehicle   36,000
    A-Cash   36,000

10. SE-Dividend declared   8,000
    A-Cash   8,000

b) Sweet Dreams Chocolatiers Ltd.: T-Accounts

A-Cash				A-Accounts receivable		
✓	0			✓	0	
(1)	200,000	440,000	(5)	(3) 650,000	580,000	(4)
(4)	580,000	24,000	(6)			
		24,000	(7)	✓ 70,000		
		46,000	(8)			
		36,000	(9)			
		8,000	(10)			
✓	202,000					

A-Inventory				A-Vehicle		
✓	0			✓	0	
(2)	460,000	380,000	(3)	(9)	36,000	
✓	80,000			✓	36,000	

L-Accounts payable				SE-Common shares		
		0	✓			0 ✓
(5)	440,000	460,000	(2)			200,000 (1)
		20,000	✓			200,000 ✓

SE-Retained earnings				SE-Dividends declared		
		0	✓	✓	0	
				(10)	8,000	
				✓	8,000	

SE-Sales			SE-Cost of goods sold		
	0	✓	✓	0	
	650,000	(3)	(3) 380,000		
	650,000	✓	✓ 380,000		

SE-Rent expense			SE-Other expenses		
✓	0		✓	0	
(6)	24,000		(7)	24,000	
✓	24,000		✓	24,000	

SE-Wages expense		
✓	0	
(8)	46,000	
✓	46,000	

c)

Sweet Dreams Chocolatiers Ltd.
Trial Balance
December 31, 20x1

	Debit	Credit
Cash	$202,000	
Accounts receivable	70,000	
Inventory	80,000	
Vehicles	36,000	
Accounts payable		$20,000
Common shares		200,000
Retained earnings		-0-
Dividends declared	8,000	
Sales		650,000
Cost of goods sold	380,000	
Rent expense	24,000	
Other expenses	24,000	
Wages expense	46,000	
	$870,000	$870,000

3-21 a) The Riders Shop Ltd.: Journal Entries

March	1	A-Cash	100,000	
		SE-Common shares		100,000
	2	SE-Rent expense	2,100	
		A-Cash		2,100
	5	A-Parts inventory	24,000	
		L-Accounts payable		24,000
	7	A-Shop supplies on hand	11,100	
		A-Cash		11,100
	9	A-Accounts receivable	530	
		SE-Sale of parts		310
		SE-Service revenue		220
		SE-Cost of parts sold	155	
		A-Parts inventory		155
	11	A-Parts inventory	750	
		A-Cash		750
	12	L-Accounts payable	24,000	
		A-Cash		24,000
	15	A-Cash	500	
		SE-Sale of parts		190
		SE-Service revenue		310
		SE-Cost of parts sold	95	
		A-Parts inventory		95
	15	SE-Wages expense	900	
		A-Cash		900

16	A-Cash	750	
	L-Advances from customers		750
	L-Advances from customers	125	
	SE-Service revenue		125
20	A-Prepaid insurance	540	
	A-Cash		540
22	A-Cash	2,246	
	SE-Sale of parts		846
	SE-Service revenue		1,400
	SE-Cost of parts sold	423	
	A-Parts inventory		423
25	A-Accounts receivable	510	
	SE-Sale of parts		510
	SE-Cost of parts sold	255	
	A-Parts inventory		255
28	A-Cash	530	
	A-Accounts receivable		530
31	SE-Wages expense	925	
	A-Cash		925

b) The Rider Shop Ltd.: T-Accounts

A-Cash					A-Accounts receivable			
✓	0				✓	0		
(1)	100,000	2,100	(2)		(9)	530	530	(28)
(15)	500	11,100	(7)		(25)	510		
(16)	750	750	(11)					
(22)	2,246	24,000	(12)		✓	510		
(28)	530	900	(15)					
		540	(20)					
		925	(31)					
✓	63,711							

A-Parts Inventory					A-Shop supplies on hand		
✓	0				✓	0	
(5)	24,000	155	(9)		(7)	11,100	
(11)	750	95	(15)				
		423	(22)		✓	11,100	
		255	(25)				
✓	23,822						

A-Prepaid insurance			
✓	0		
(20)	540		
		0	
	540		

L-Accounts payable

		0	✓
(12)	24,000	24,000	(5)
		0	✓

L-Advances from customers

		0	✓
(16)	125	750	(16)
		625	✓

SE-Common shares

	0	✓
	100,000	(1)
	100,000	✓

SE-Retained earnings

	0 ✓
	0

SE-Sale of parts

	0	✓
	310	(9)
	190	(15)
	846	(22)
	510	(25)
	1,856	✓

SE-Service revenue

0	✓ ✓	
	220	(9)
	310	(15)
	125	(16)
	1,400	(22)
	2,055	✓

SE-Cost of parts sold

0	
(9)	155
(15)	95
(22)	423
(25)	255
✓	928

SE-Wages expense		
✓	0	
(15)	900	
(31)	925	
✓	1,825	

SE-Rent expense		
	✓	0
(2)	2,100	
✓	2,100	

c)

Riders Shop Ltd.
Trial Balance
March 31, 20x1

	Debit	Credit
Cash	$ 63,711	
Accounts receivable	510	
Parts inventory	23,822	
Shop supplies on hand	11,100	
Prepaid insurance	540	
Advances from customers		$ 625
Common shares		100,000
Retained earnings		-0-
Sales of parts		1,856
Service revenue		2,055
Cost of parts sold	928	
Wages expense	1,825	
Rent expense	2,100	
	$104,536	$104,536

d)

Riders Shop Ltd.
Income Statement
For the month ending March 31, 20x1

Sales of parts	$1,856	
Service revenue	2,055	
Total revenue		$3,911
Expenses		
Cost of parts sold	$ 928	
Wages expense	1,825	
Rent expense		2,100
Total expenses		4,853
Net loss		$(942)

Riders Shop Ltd.
Balance Sheet
As at March 31, 20x1

Assets
    Cash $63,711
    Accounts receivable   510
    Parts inventory   23,822
    Shop supplies on hand   11,100
    Prepaid insurance   540
Total assets $99,683

Liabilities
    Advances from customers $ 625
Shareholders' equity
    Common shares   100,000
    Retained earnings   (942)
Total shareholders' equity   99,058
Total liabilities and shareholders'
    Equity $99,683

3-23 1) Hughes Tool Company: Journal Entries

1.	A–Cash	120,000	
	SE–Common shares		120,000
2.	A–Cash	300,000	
	L–Bank loan payable		300,000
3.	SE–Rent expense	80,000	
	A – Prepaid Rent	20,000	
	A – Cash		100,000

4. A–Equipment   240,000
        A–Cash   240,000
    SE–Amortization expense   30,000
        XA–Accum. amort.   30,000
        [($240,000 – 30,000)/7 years = $30,000]

5. A–Inventory   100,000
        A–Cash   100,000

6. A–Cash   80,000
    A–Accounts receivable   720,000
        SE–Sales revenue   800,000

7. A–Cash   640,000
        A–Accounts receivable   640,000

8. A–Inventory   550,000
        L–Accounts payable   550,000

9. L–Accounts Payable   495,000
        A–Cash   495,000

10. SE–Cost of goods sold   535,000
        A – Inventory   535,000
    Cost of Goods Sold is calculated as:
    Beginning Balance + Purchases – Ending Balance =
    $100,000 + 550,000 – 115,000 =$535,000

11. SE–Dividend declared   40,000
        A–Cash   40,000

12. SE–Interest expense   36,000
    L–Bank loan payable   20,000
        A–Cash   56,000
        ($300,000 X 12% = $36,000)

13. SE–Selling and administrative
                expense   90,000
        A–Cash   80,000
        L–Accrued expenses   10,000

14. SE–Tax expense   8,700
        A–Cash   6,525
        L–Income Tax Payable   2,175

The tax calculation is based on the income before taxes of $29,000 (see the income statement for Problem 2-34) multiplied by the tax rate of 30% or $8,700. The amount paid in cash is then determined by multiplying by 75%.

2) Hughes Tool Company: T-Accounts

A-Cash				A- Accounts Receivable			
	0				0		
(1)	120,000	100,000	(3)	(6) 720,000	640,000	(7)	
(2)	300,000	240,000	(4)				
(6)	80,000	100,000	(5)	80,000			
(7)	640,000	495,000	(9)				
		40,000	(11)				
		56,000	(12)				
		80,000	(13)				
		6,525	(14)				
	22,475						

A-Inventory				A- Prepaid Rent			
	0				0		
(5)	100,000			(3)	20,000		
(8)	550,000	535,000	(10)				
	115,000				20,000		

A-Equipment			XA-Accum. amort.	
	0			0
(4) 240,000				30,000 (4)
240,000				30,000

L- Accounts Payable			L-Accrued expenses	
	0			0
(9) 495,000	550,000 (8)			10,000 (13)
	55,000			10,000

L-Income tax payable			L-Bank Loan Payable	
	0			0
	2,175 (14)		(12) 20,000	300,000 (2)
	2,175			280,000

SE-Common shares			SE-Retained earnings	
	0			0
	120,000 (1)		(I) 40,000	20,300 (H)
	120,000		19,700	

SE-Dividend declared			SE-Sales revenue	
	0			0
(11) 40,000	40,000 (I)		(A) 800,000	800,000 (6)
	0			0

SE-Cost of goods sold

		0		
(10)	535,000	535,000	(B)
		0	

SE-Rent expense

		0		
(3)	80,000	80,000	(C)
		0	

SE-Amortization expense

		0		
(4)	30,000	30,000	(D)
		0	

SE-Interest expense

		0		
(12)	36,000	36,000	(E)
		0	

SE-Selling & admin. expense

		0		
(13)	90,000	90,000	(F)
		0	

SE-Tax expense

		0		
(14)	8,700	8,700	(G)
		0	

SE-Income Summary

		0		
(B)	535,000	800,000	(A)
(C)	80,000		
(D)	30,000		
(E)	36,000		
(F)	90,000		
(G)	8,700		
(H)	20,300	20,300	
		0	

3)

Hughes Tool Company
Trial Balance
September 30, 20x4

	Debit	Credit
Cash	$ 22,475	
Accounts receivable	80,000	
Inventory	115,000	
Prepaid rent	20,000	
Equipment	240,000	
Accumulated amortization		$ 30,000
Accounts payable		55,000
Accrued expenses		10,000
Bank loan payable		280,000
Income tax payable		2,175
Common shares		120,000
Retained earnings		-0-
Dividend declared	40,000	
Sales revenue		800,000
Cost of goods sold	535,000	
Rent expense	80,000	
Amortization expense	30,000	
Interest expense	36,000	
Selling & administrative expenses	90,000	
Tax expense	8,700	
	$1,297,175	$1,297,175

4) Closing Entries

	Debit	Credit
A. SE–Sales revenue	800,000	
SE–Income summary		800,000
B. SE–Income summary	535,000	
SE–Cost of goods sold		535,000
C. SE–Income summary	80,000	
SE–Rent expense		80,000

D. SE–Income summary	30,000	
SE–Amortization expense		30,000
E. SE–Income summary	36,000	
SE–Interest expense		36,000
F. SE–Income summary	90,000	
SE–Selling and admini-		
strative expense		90,000
G. SE–Income summary	8,700	
SE–Tax expense		8,700
H. SE–Income summary	20,300	
SE–Retained earnings		20,300
I. SE–Retained earnings	40,000	
SE–Dividend declared		40,000

3-25

1)	Sales	$ 8,300	
2)	COGS	(2,700)	
3)	Interest income	40	
4)	Rent expense	(600)	
5)	Utility expense	(198)	(last month's utility bill of $250 should have appeared on last month's income statement)
6)	Wages expense	(350)	
7)	Other expenses	(990)	
		$ 3,502	

3-27

	September expense	October expense
1)	$4,800 ($8,000 x 3/5)	$3,200 ($8,000 x 2/5)
2)	$900	$1,000
3)	$45	$45
4)	$1,400 ($2,100 x 4 weeks/6 weeks)	$700 ($2,100 x 2 weeks/6 weeks)

3-29 a) On the Go Pizza: Journal Entries

1.	A-Cash	480,000	
	A-Accounts receivable	50,000	
	SE-Sales		530,000
2.	A-Supplies inventory	220,000	
	A-Cash		220,000
3.	SE-Cost of supplies used	215,000	
	A-Supplies inventory		215,000
4.	L-Wages payable	4,000	
	SE-Wage expense	71,000	
	A-Cash		75,000
5.	SE-Other expenses	52,000	
	A-Cash		52,000
6.	A-Cash	52,000	
	A-Accounts receivable		52,000
7.	SE-Dividends declared	10,000	
	A-Cash		10,000

b) On the Go Pizza: T-Accounts

A-Cash

✓	150,000		
(1)	480,000	220,000	(2)
(6)	52,000	75,000	(4)
		52,000	(5)
		10,000	(7)
	325,000		

A-Accounts receivable

✓	5,000		
(1)	50,000	52,000	(6)
	3,000		

A-Supplies inventory

✓	15,000		
(2)	220,000	215,000	(3)
	20,000		

A-Prepaid rent

✓	36,000		
		18,000	(9)
	18,000		

A-Equipment

✓	60,000	
	60,000	

XA-Accum. amort. – equip.

	0	✓
	7,500	(10)
	7,500	

A-Delivery vehicle

✓	80,000	
	80,000	

XA-Accum. amort. – del. veh.

	0	✓
	15,000	(11)
	15,000	

L-Wages payable

		4,000	✓
(4)	4,000		
		0	
		2,000	(8)
		2,000	

SE-Common shares

Debit	Credit	
	200,000	✓
	200,000	

SE–Retained earnings

Debit		Credit	
		142,000	✓
		142,000	
(H)	10,000	149,500	(G)
		281,500	

SE-Income summary

Debit		Credit	
		0	
(B)	215,000	530,000	(A)
(C)	73,000		
(D)	52,000		
(E)	18,000		
(F)	22,500		
		149,500	
(G)	149,500		
		0	

SE–Dividends declared

	Debit	Credit	
✓	0		
(6)	10,000		
	10,000	10,000	(H)
	0		

SE-Sales

Debit		Credit	
		0	✓
		530,000	(1)
(A)	530,000	530,000	
		0	

SE-Cost of supplies used

	Debit	Credit	
✓	0		
(3)	215,000		
	215,000	215,000	(B)
	0		

SE-Wages expense

	Debit	Credit	
✓	0		
(4)	71,000		
	71,000		
(8)	2,000		
	73,000	73,000	(C)
	0		

SE–Other expense

	Debit	Credit	
✓	0		
(5)	52,000		
	52,000	52,000	(D)
	0		

SE-Rent expense		
✓	0	
(9)	18,000	
	18,000	18,000 (E)
	0	

SE–Amortization expense		
✓	0	
(10)	7,500	
(11)	15,000	
	22,500	22,500 (F)
	0	

c)

On the Go Pizza
Trial Balance
December 31, 20x2

	Debit	Credit
Cash	$ 325,000	
Accounts receivable	3,000	
Supplies inventory	20,000	
Prepaid rent	18,000	
Equipment	60,000	
Accumulated amortization – equip.		$ 7,500
Delivery vehicles	80,000	
Accumulated amortization – del.veh.		15,000
Wages payable		2,000
Common shares		200,000
Retained earnings		142,000
Dividend declared	10,000	
Sales		530,000
Cost of supplies used	215,000	
Wages expense	73,000	
Other expense	52,000	
Rent expense	18,000	
Amortization expense	22,500	
	$896,500	$896,500

d) Adjusting entries

8. SE-Wages expense   2,000
       L-Wages payable   2,000

9. SE-Rent expense   18,000
       A-Prepaid rent   18,000

10. SE-Amortization expense   7,500
       XA-Accum. amort. – equip.   7,500
       ($60,000 / 8 = $7,500)

11. SE-Amortization expense   15,000
       XA-Accum. amort. – del.veh.   15,000
       [($80,000 - $5,000)/5 = $15,000]

e)

On the Go Pizza
Income Statement
For the year ended December 31, 20x2

Sales		$530,000
Expenses		
Cost of supplies used	$215,000	
Wages expense	73,000	
Other expense	52,000	
Rent expense	18,000	
Amortization expense	22,500	
Total expenses		380,500
Net income		$149,500

On the Go Pizza
Balance Sheet
As at December 31, 20x2

Assets
Current assets
Cash		$ 325,000
Accounts receivable		3,000
Supplies inventory		20,000
Prepaid rent		18,000
Total current assets		366,000
Equipment	$60,000	
Less accumulated amortization	(7,500)	52,500
Delivery vehicles	80,000	
Less accumulated amortization	15,000	65,000
Total noncurrent assets		117,500
Total assets		$483,500

Liabilities
Wages payable		$ 2,000
Shareholders' equity		
Common shares	$200,000	
Retained earnings*	281,500	
Total shareholders' equity		481,500
Total liabilities & shareholders' equity		$483,500

*$142,000 + 149,500 − 10,000 = $281,500

f) Closing entries

A. SE-Sales	530,000	
SE-Income summary		530,000
B. SE-Income summary	215,000	
SE-Cost of supplies used		215,000
C. SE-Income summary	73,000	
SE-Wages expense		73,000

| D. SE-Income summary | 52,000 | |
| SE-Other expense | | 52,000 |

| E. SE-Income summary | 18,000 | |
| SE-Rent expense | | 18,000 |

| F. SE-Income summary | 22,500 | |
| SE-Amortization expense | | 22,500 |

| G. SE-Income summary | 149,500 | |
| SE-Retained earnings | | 149,500 |

| H. SE-Retained earnings | 10,000 | |
| SE-Dividends declared | | 10,000 |

3-31 a) Genesis Sportswear Ltd. : Journal entries

| 1. A-Cash | 40,000 | |
| SE-Common shares | | 40,000 |

| 2. A-Prepaid insurance | 1,200 | |
| A-Cash | | 1,200 |

| 3. A-Inventory | 18,500 | |
| L-Accounts payable | | 18,500 |

| 4. A-Inventory | 26,900 | |
| A-Cash | | 26,900 |

| 5. A-Accounts receivable | 85,000 | |
| SE-Sales | | 85,000 |

| 6. A-Cash | 76,000 | |
| A-Accounts receivable | | 76,000 |

| 7. SE-Cost of goods sold | 41,800 | |
| A-Inventory | | 41,800 |

8. L-Accounts payable   17,100
      A-Cash   17,100

9. A-Equipment   11,000
      A-Cash   11,000

10. SE-Dividends declared   1,300
      L-Dividend payable   1,300

b) Genesis Sportswear Ltd.: T-Accounts

A-Cash			
(1)	40,000	1,200	(2)
(6)	76,000	26,900	(4)
		17,100	(8)
		11,000	(9)
	59,800		

A-Accounts receivable			
(5)	85,000	76,000	(6)
	9,000		

A-Inventory			
(3)	18,500	41,800	(7)
(4)	26,900		
	3,600		

A-Prepaid insurance			
(2)	1,200		
	1,200	600	(11)
	600		

A-Equipment			
(9)	11,000		
	11,000		

XA-Accum. amort. – equip.		
	4,500	(12)
	4,500	

L-Accounts payable			
(8)	17,100	18,500	(3)
		1,400	

L-Dividend payable		
	1,300	(10)
	1,300	

SE-Common shares

	40,000	(1)
	40,000	

SE–Retained earnings

(C)	1,300	38,100	(B)	
		36,800		

SE-Income summary

(B)	38,100	38,100	(A)	
		0		

SE–Dividends declared

(10)	1,300			
	1,300	1,300	(C)	
	0			

SE-Sales

		85,000	(5)	
(A)	85,000	85,000		
		0		

SE-Cost of goods sold

(7)	41,800			
	41,800	41,800	(A)	
	0			

SE-Insurance expense

(11)	600			
	600	600	(A)	
	0			

SE–Amortization expense

(12)	4,500			
	4,500	4,500	(A)	
	0			

c)

Genesis Sportswear Ltd.
Trial Balance
December 31, 20xx

	Debit	Credit
Cash	$59,800	
Accounts receivable	9,000	
Inventory	3,600	
Prepaid insurance	1,200	
Equipment	11,000	
Accounts payable		$1,400
Dividend payable		1,300
Common shares		40,000
Dividend declared	1,300	
Sales		85,000
Cost of goods sold	41,800	
	$127,700	$127,700

d) Adjusting entries

11. SE-Insurance expense	600	
A-Prepaid insurance		600
12. SE-Amortization expense	4,500	
XA-Accumulated amort.		4,500

Genesis Sportswear Ltd.
Adjusted Trial Balance
December 31, 20xx

	Debit	Credit
Cash	$59,800	
Accounts receivable	9,000	
Inventory	3,600	
Prepaid insurance	600	
Equipment	11,000	
Accumulated amortization		$4,500

Accounts payable		1,400
Dividend payable		1,300
Common shares		40,000
Dividend declared	1,300	
Sales		85,000
Cost of goods sold	41,800	
Insurance expense	600	
Amortization expense	4,500	
	$132,200	$132,200

e) Closing entries

A.	SE-Sales	85,000	
	SE-Cost of goods sold		41,800
	SE-Insurance expense		600
	SE-Amortization expense		4,500
	SE-Income summary		38,100
B.	SE-Income summary	38,100	
	SE-Retained earnings		38,100
C.	SE-Retained earnings	1,300	
	SE-Dividends declared		1,300

3-33 Cozy Fireplaces Inc.: Adjusting entries

1.	SE-Sales	3,100	
	L-Deposits from customers		3,100
2.	SE-Interest expense	2,667	
	L-Interest payable		2,667
	($40,000x8%x10/12 = $2,667)		
3.	SE-Salaries and wages expense	2,200	
	L-Salaries payable		2,200

4. A-Prepaid rent   1,000

     SE-Rent expense   1,000

5. SE-Office supplies used   7,000

     A-Office supplies   7,000

6. SE-Amortization expense   5,000

     XA-Accumulated amortization   5,000

7. SE-Income tax expense*   59,410

     L-Income tax payable   59,410

*Sales	846,900
Cost of goods sold	(480,000)
Salaries and wages expense	(97,200)
Miscellaneous expense	(15,000)
Rent expense	(42,000)
Office supplies used	(7,000)
Interest expense	(2,667)
Amortization expense	(5,000)
Net income	$198,033

($198,033 x 30% = $59,410)

3-35 **a)** Increase assets (inventory) and decrease assets (cash)

b) Increase assets (framing supplies) and increase liabilities (accounts payable)

c) Decrease assets (cash) and decrease liabilities (bank loan)

d) Increase assets (cash), increase shareholders' equity (revenue)

e) Decrease shareholders' equity (cost of goods sold), decrease assets (inventory)

f) Decrease assets (inventory) and decrease shareholders' equity (loss due to breakage)

g) Increase assets (cash) and decrease assets (accounts receivable)

h) Decrease assets (cash) and decrease liabilities (accounts payable)

Biggs & Company Ltd.
Income Statement
For the year ended December 31, 2003

Income from regular operations:

Sales revenue	$195,000	
Cost of goods sold	(125,000)	
Gross profit	70,000	
Operating expenses	(45,000)	
Income from regular operations		$25,000

Income (loss) from non-operating sources:

Interest expense	(5,000)	
Dividend revenue	500	
Gain on the sale of land	1,200	
Loss due to windstorm damage	(2,300)	
Income from non-operating sources		(5,600)
Income before income tax		19,400
Provision for income tax (Income tax expense)		(7,760)
Income before discontinued operations and extraordinary items		11,640
Loss on discontinued operations $32,000, net of tax saving of $12,800		(19,200)
Income (loss) before extraordinary items		(7,560)
Loss due to earthquake damage $4,500, net of tax of $1,800	(2,700)	
Gain on expropriation of land $6,000, net of tax of $2,400	3,600	
Gain (loss) from extraordinary items (net of tax)		900
Net income (loss)		($6,660)

Note: Dividends Declared are not an expense; they are part of the calculation of Retained Earnings.

USER PERSPECTIVE SOLUTIONS

3-39 There are incentives for companies to speed up the accounting closing process. Management and external users of financial statements need up-to-date information in order to make decisions. Such information cannot be useful if it is not provided on a timely basis. Thus, pressure from financial statement users is one incentive for companies to speed up the process. Also, sophisticated computer systems have decreased the costs of closing the books, making it easier for companies to speed up this process.

3-41 This policy is very prudent. The main objective in preparing financial statements is to provide information for users' decisions. If users do not understand the financial statements they cannot hope to make informed decisions as they will not be able to assess the risk of their proposed investment.

Advantages of the proposed strategy:
- Avoid unwise business investments due to lack of understanding of company's financial situation
- Encourage companies to improve financial disclosure and understandability of their financial statements, in order to attract investors

Disadvantages of proposed strategy:
- Potential loss of good investment opportunities
- Investors may give up quickly if financial statements are not easily understandable rather than doing background investigation to improve their understanding

3-43 a)

Northland Enterprises
Income Statement
For the year ending December 31, 20x2

Income from continuing operations:
Operating revenues:

Equipment sales	$6,500,000	
Sales of replacement parts	900,000	
Repair revenue	700,000	$8,100,000

Operating expenses:

Cost of parts and equipment	4,200,000	
Wages and salaries	1,000,000	
Shipping and delivery costs	690,000	5,890,000
Income from continuing operations		2,210,000

Income from nonoperating sources:
Financing revenue

Interest income	70,000	

Financing expenses

Interest expense	(90,000)	
Property taxes	(100,000)	
Income from nonoperating sources		(120,000)
Income before income tax		2,090,000
Income tax expense		730,000
Net income		$1,360,000

b) For 2001, a net income of $1,360,000 is reported and the
return on total revenue is 16.79%. Northland's net income
goal has been reached, but it failed to achieve a 20% return
on total revenue.

c) In setting its goals for net income and return on sales for
future periods, Northland should consider items that enter
into the determination of net income that are infrequent or
might not occur in future years. Although there were no
discontinued operations or extraordinary items for 20x2, the
effects of such occurrences, had some existed, should be
deducted in setting goals for future years.

Other factors that Northland should consider are
expected growth trends for sales, the effect of new product

lines on sales, the impact of any discontinued product lines, competitors' actions, predicted weather patterns (impact on snowmobile sales), and changes in cost structure (increased efficiencies? supplier costs ↑? wage negotiations?)

READING AND INTERPRETING PUBLISHED FINANCIAL STATEMENTS SOLUTIONS

3-45 a) Sears Canada has used a single-step income statement. It combines cost of merchandise sold, operating, administrative and selling expenses, making it impossible to determine gross profit. Also, it does not separate any of the other expenses into operating and financing, which is common of a single-step income statement.

b) It means that Sears Canada has some securities (e.g. stock options, convertible bonds, or preferred shares) that could increase the number of common shares outstanding. However, if these securities are converted in the future, the additional number of shares will not negatively affect the earnings per share, as the earnings per share for both calculations is $0.88 in 2001.

c) The two largest assets on the balance sheet at December 29, 2001 are capital assets, $1,188.7 million (30.6% of total assets) and accounts receivable of $871.9 million (22.5%). This is reasonable as Sears Canada operates retail stores (an investment in land, buildings, and fixtures). The accounts receivable represents amounts owing from customers and is approximately 13% of total revenues, representing about one and a half months worth of sales (assuming sales earned evenly). Inventory is the third largest asset, $864.5 million (22.3% of total assets). This represents the value of goods held for resale.

3-47 a) Intrawest Corporation has used a multi-step income statement. Income and expense items are segregated for each operating line and corporate, general, and administrative expenses are shown separately. Gross profit is determinable for each of the main business segments.

b)

	2001	2000
Revenue: Ski and Resort operations	$492,202	$447,350
Expenses: Ski and Resort operations	383,864	353,662
Gross Profit	$108,338	$ 93,688
Revenue: Real estate sales	$415,336	$341,455
Expenses: Real estate sales	338,856	281,845
Gross Profit	$ 76,480	$ 59,610
Revenue: Rental properties	$8,935	$6,905
Expenses: Rental properties	4,426	3,641
Gross Profit	$4,509	$3,264

Gross profit increased for all three business segments from 2000 to 2001.

c) Discontinued operations are operations of an identifiable business segment that have been sold, shut down, abandoned, or otherwise disposed of, or is subject to a formal plan of disposal. Discontinued operations are shown at the end of the income statement to ensure clarity when analyzing potential future cash flows from continuing operations. Discontinued operations are shown net of tax. Tax from continuing operations is shown before net income from continuing operations. Discontinued operations are shown after net income from continuing operations, so they must include their portion of tax.

d) Intrawest shows two earnings per share (EPS) amounts; Income per share from continuing operations and Income per share on net income (after discontinued operations). Among other things, users would want to see EPS from continuing operations in evaluating the ongoing future potential of the firm. They would want to see EPS after discontinued operations in evaluating the performance of the overall investment.

BEYOND THE BOOK SOLUTIONS

3-49 Answers to this question will depend on the company selected.

CHAPTER 4

Revenue Recognition

ASSESSING YOUR RECAL SOLUTIONS

4-1 ROI measures performance by expressing the return from an investment as a proportion of the average amount invested. In order to measure return, businesses need to determine the change in assets and liabilities from one period to the next. This is accomplished through the income statement.

4-3 The three main criteria of revenue recognition are that the revenue be earned, that the amount earned can be measured, and that there is reasonable assurance that the amounts earned will be collected.

4-5 The percentage of completion method recognizes revenues (and the related expenses) based on the fraction of work that is done during the current period. The fraction of work completed during the period is usually estimated by the costs incurred relative to the total estimated costs to complete the project. The completed contracts method, on the other hand, postpones the recognition of revenue (and expense) until the project is completed. All revenues and expenses are then recognized at the end of the construction period when the project is delivered to the customer.

4-7 The matching principle simply states that when revenues are recognized, all costs necessary to generate those revenues should be matched with the revenues as expenses on the income statement.

APPLYING YOUR KNOWLEDGE SOLUTIONS

4-9 Advertising revenue is recognized as soon as the advertisement is printed in an issue of the magazine. At this point, the company has completed its commitment to the customer; it printed the advertisement. It knows how much it has earned and it can estimate the collectibility of the amount.
The subscription revenue is recognized as each issue is sent. At this point, the company has completed its part of the contract; it sent the issue. It has probably already collected the subscription amount from the customer, so both the amount and collectibility are known.

4-11

a) Return $210,000 - $180,000 $30,000
Average investment $180,000
ROI   16.67%

b) Return $4,000
Average investment $110,000
ROI   3.64%

c) Return $3.75 x 5,000 $18,750
Average investment $20,000
ROI   93.75%

d) Return   10 x ($8.10 - $6.60) $15
Average investment   10 x $6.60 $66
ROI   22.73%

e) Return $120,000
Average investment ($1,340,000+1,150,000)/2 $1,245,000
ROI   9.64%

4-13

Tinder Box Furnace Company
Income Statement
For the Year ending December 31, 2004

Sales	($1,230,000 - $65,000)	$1,165,000
Cost of Goods Sold	($580,000 + $245,000)	(825,000)
Gross Profit		340,000
Warranty expense		65,000
Net income		$275,000

4-15 Gross profit % = ($450 - $225) / $450 = 50%

Month	Accounts Receivable	Unearned profit	Profit
1	$360	$180	$45
2	$270	$135	$45
3	$180	$90	$45
4	$90	$45	$45
5	$0	$0	$45

4-17 a) 1. Percentage of completion method

Year		Revenue (millions)	Expense (millions)	Profit (millions)
1	(21.2 / 96) x 120	$ 26.5	$21.2	$ 5.3
2	(36.4 / 96) x 120	$ 45.5	$36.4	$ 9.1
3	(26.0 / 96) x 120	$ 32.5	$26.0	$ 6.5
4	(12.4 / 96) x 120	$ 15.5	$12.4	$ 3.1
		$120.0	$96.0	$24.0

2. Completed contract method

Year	Revenue (millions)	Expense (millions)	Profit (millions)
1	0	0	0
2	0	0	0
3	0	0	0
4	$120	$96	$24
	$120	$96	$24

b) The percentage of completion method should be used to indicate the performance of Cruise Shipping Inc. under the contract because the revenue is earned over the course of the contract rather than all at once upon completion. Since the work is done over a four-year period, the percentage of completion method is most appropriate. If the collectibility of the amount was in question, using the completed contract method would be more appropriate.

4-19 a) Percentage of completion method

Year		Revenue (millions)	Expense (millions)	Profit (millions)
2003	(220.75 / 800) x 1,500,000	$413,906	$220,750	$193,156
2004	(400.5/800) x 1,500,000	$750,938	$400,500	$350,438
2005	(178.75/800) x 1,500,000	$335,156	$178,750	$156,406
		$1,500,000	$800,000	$700,000

b) The percentage of completion method should be used because the revenue is earned over the course of the contract rather than all at once upon completion. Since the work is done over several periods, the percentage of completion method is most appropriate. If the collectibility of the amount earned were in question, using the completed contract method would be more appropriate.

4-21 Jocelyn Black should recognize revenue when she delivers the food, which will likely be the same date as the function itself. Once the food has been delivered (the function has occurred) the revenue has been earned because Jocelyn has completed her responsibilities. Thus, the first revenue recognition criteria has been met.

　　The second revenue recognition criteria, the amount earned can be measured, is also met. Jocelyn's records will indicate the price negotiated with the customer, as she will likely have provided each customer with a written price quote, or have a brochure with standard prices listed. Her records will also provide details of costs incurred: food and labour costs (based on hours incurred).

　　Currently, there is reasonable assurance of collectibility at the time food is delivered, as Jocelyn has not previously experienced problems with non-payment. So the third revenue recognition criteria is also met. However, as her business expands, Jocelyn may need to estimate an expense to deal with the possibility of non-payment by customers. As long as she is able to make a reasonable estimate of this expense, she can continue to recognize revenue at time of food delivery. The estimated expense of non-payment will be matched to revenue at that time.

4-23 a) Terry has two separate cash-to-cash cycles. The speculative design business has cash outflows while the games are being developed, then has cash inflows only if the games are sold. The custom design business has a much shorter cash-to-cash cycle, with monthly cash outflows and monthly or less frequent cash inflows coming in after the invoices for the work are sent out.

b) Terry could recognize revenues at the time of sale, at the time of contract signing, at the time of production, or at the time of collection of cash. For the speculative design, the time of sale basis would provide the best information, as until the games are sold, there is no certainty of any revenue. For hourly rate custom design, the percentage of completion basis (production) may be appropriate as Terry has a paying customer up front and the revenue is earned on an hourly basis as the work is done. However, if the work is normally completed within a short period of time, recognizing revenue when the work is complete would be simpler and would not lead to materially different results.

c) Accounting for costs incurred would depend on the kind of business. For speculative games, all costs incurred would be deferred as inventory assets until the games are sold, at which time the costs would be recognized as expenses to match to the revenues being earned. If Terry finds that any speculative games are found to be not saleable, the cost associated with those games would be recognized as expenses. For custom designs, Terry would either recognize costs as they are incurred (for the hourly rate contracts) or defer the costs until the project is completed (for the fixed fee contracts). In all cases, costs should be matched with revenue.

d) The main difficulties with this business appear to be the requirement that a stream of games be continually produced and that the cash flows need to be controlled. We should recommend that Terry produce a cash budget showing all expected cash inflows and outflows, as a continual supply of cash will be needed to be able to assure a continual flow of new games that can be marketed. We might recommend that Terry try to achieve a steady custom design business to produce the cash needed to fund the speculative designs. Terry might also try to convince Kim to accept the same type of contract that Sandy has for the speculative game design in order to reduce the required cash outflows for wages.

USER PERSPECTIVE SOLUTIONS

4-25 If a company is thinking of going public, it might have an incentive to misstate its income statement via its revenue recognition policies. For example, if it recognizes revenue earlier in the cash-to-cash cycle, it can increase its net income and attract a higher price from the share issuance. If a company did change its revenue recognition policy in order to enhance earnings, investors should realize what it is doing from its financial statements and related notes. Changes in accounting policy as well as the effects of such changes on net income must be disclosed in the notes to the financial statements, according to GAAP.

4-27 I would recommend that the company count a sale when it ships the goods, as long as a reasonable estimate can be made of the possibility of non-payment by the customer. Such an estimate is not likely to be a problem for a large company due to its past experience with customer collections.

I would not wait until the company receives payment unless I had reason to suspect that sales were being made to marginal customers with a high risk of non-payment. This could be a danger if my sales people are so motivated by the incentive plan that they are foregoing the company's usual customer credit investigation policies.

I would not count revenue when the sales person generates a purchase order. Although it can be argued that this is closer to the time when the sales person has expended the effort to "sell" the customer and thus provides a more timely measure of sales people's performance, the first revenue recognition criteria has not been met. Until the goods are shipped, the company has not fully earned the revenue (fulfilled their responsibility to the customer).

4-29 It might be appropriate for the toy company to recognize revenue at the time of shipment as long as it could reliably estimate the impact of returns. Just as you would estimate bad debts, the toy company must estimate and record an allowance for sales returns. To record revenues without any recognition of the effect of sales returns would not be appropriate since all of the revenues would not have been earned. If there is high uncertainty as to the amount of toys that might be returned, then the uncertainties of realizing the revenues would be such that the company should not record revenues at time of shipment. Consignment sales are typical of this nature where title does not pass to the buyer but resides with the seller until the goods are ultimately sold to the final consumer.

4-31 I would recognize revenue from the monthly rent payments at the end of the month in which they are paid. At that time I have earned the revenue (provided the service) and the amount earned is known and collected. All revenue recognition criteria are met. For example, rent received on March 1 could be recorded as a liability (customer prepayment/unearned revenue) when received, and recorded as revenue on March 31. However, if I am unlikely to need to prepare financial statements during a month, I could take a shortcut and record the March 1 rent payment as March revenue, when received.

  The damage deposit collected would be recorded as a liability also, and would remain so until the tenant vacated the apartment. At that time the damage deposit would either be returned [debit Damage Deposit (L), credit Cash (A)] or recorded as revenue at that time [debit Damage Deposit (L), credit Revenue (SE)]. In the latter case, the revenue is matched against the costs of repairing the apartment.

  The one-year lease does not affect my revenue recognition decision, which depends on the revenue recognition criteria and adherence to the matching principle.

4-33 Although the cash has been received, the criteria for revenue recognition have not been satisfied because the GAP still bears the risks of owning the merchandise and must fulfill its obligation to holders of the gift certificates. Thus, the gift certificates should be recognized in the financial statements as unearned revenue (a liability).

4-35 Old inventory suggests that it is either damaged or obsolete. In either case it is not likely to generate revenues in the future and should therefore not be considered an asset on the books of the company. The company should write-off the cost of the inventory, which will reduce the balance sheet value of inventory and increase the cost of the inventory (the cost of goods sold), or it might be reported as a loss separate from the cost of goods sold. Management may have been keeping the inventory so as to avoid the negative impact on the income statement, particularly if the amount was significant. There could be numerous reasons for this, one of which might be that management is compensated based on a bonus plan which is calculated based on reported net income.

READING AND INTERPRETING PUBLISHED FINANCIAL STATEMENTS SOLUTIONS

4-37 Companies such as Eddie Bauer incur catalogue costs in order to generate mail-order sales revenue. The matching concept would seem to indicate that these costs should be matched against the revenues that are generated from the catalogue. These expenses should probably be deferred and recognized over the period for which the catalogue is effective to best match revenues and expenses.

4-39 a) There are three specific criteria to be considered before revenue can be recognized. The first factor is whether the revenue has been earned. Revenue is considered to have been earned when the company has substantially completed what it must do to be entitled to the benefits of the revenue. For the earnings process to be substantially complete, the company has completed most of what it agreed to do and there are very few costs yet to be incurred in the cash-to-cash cycle, and that these costs are subject to reasonable estimation. Another way is to consider this factor is to think about whether the risks and rewards of the goods been transferred to the seller. IPSCO is a steel manufacturer. The completion of the steel fabrication process could reasonably be considered as substantial completion, as shipping the finished goods is not a major part of the process and the costs of shipping, if borne by IPSCO, can be reasonably estimated

The second recognition criteria is measurement. Steel manufacturing is generally completed under contract for a set price that is clearly measurable.

The third revenue recognition criteria is assurance that payment is collectable. Large steel manufacturers typically deal with large well-known clients. Collection is reasonably assured and/or a provision for losses can be set up based on past lost experience.

IPSCO's revenue recognition policy meets all three recognition requirements

b) IPSCO has likely specified acceptance of or shipment of products in order to recognize revenue as quickly as possible. Shipping of steel product often involves significant logistics. If the product is not scheduled to be shipped for a period of time but the buyer accepts the product, ownership transfers when the fabrication is complete and therefore revenue can be recognized. If the product is shipped but will not be received for some period of time, ownership is set as F.O.B. IPSCO and revenue can be recognized as soon as goods are shipped. F.O.B. goods may be subject to receipt and final approval, but shipments can be insured or provision made for possible damage or defect noticed upon receipt.

4-41 If earning revenues occurs over a long period of time, the percentage of completion method is appropriate. It recognizes revenue in the time period in which the service is being provided rather than recognizing all revenue in the period when the service is finally completed. It is likely that the Canadian Pacific Railway Limited has many long-term contracts for providing railway transportation services. Thus, to accurately measure the company's performance in a particular time period, a portion of the contract revenue should be recognized proportional to the number of freight miles traveled in the period compared to the total freight miles under the contract.

It is likely that Canadian Pacific charges its customers partially based on the number of miles travelled (as well as for volume and weight of transported goods). Also, the number of miles a particular shipment has travelled at any point in time would be easy to determine, since Canadian Pacific Railway would track the location of railcars, and the distance between links is fixed. Thus the percentage of completed service method would be easily applied. At the end of an accounting period, the company could determine the distance traveled so far on shipments still in transit, and take this proportion of the total distance under the contract as revenue.

BEYOND THE BOOK SOLUTIONS

4-43 Answers to this question will depend on the company selected.

CHAPTER 5

Cash Flow Statement

ASSESSING YOUR RECALL SOLUTIONS

5-1 Because income recognition is done on an accrual basis, the recognition of revenues and expenses either leads or lags cash inflows and outflows to some degree. Therefore, the income statement is not as useful in determining the cash situation of the company. Since cash is such an important commodity and the company cannot operate without an adequate supply of it, the cash flow statement provides useful information to the user. The cash flow statement also reports on activities not covered (or partially covered) by the income statement (investment and financing activities).

5-3 The lead/lag relationship means that the cash flows of the company, for expenses and revenues, may either lead or lag the recognition of these expenses and revenues for income statement purposes. For this reason, the cash flow statement provides different information from the income statement.

5-5 The three major categories of cash flows are:
Operating Activities – These cash flows are those associated with the daily operations of the company in selling goods and services to customers.
Financing Activities – These cash flows are those associated with raising funds (cash) for the company to operate. These funds come from two major sources: debtholders and shareholders. Repayments to the debtholders (principal repayments) and shareholders (repurchase of shares and dividends) are also shown in this section.

Investing Activities – These cash flows are associated with the long-term investment of cash. The two major categories of items that fit in this section are the investment in property, plant, and equipment and the investment in other companies through acquisitions.

5-7   Amortization is not a source of cash. Cash flows related to property, plant, and equipment occur when the property, plant, and equipment is purchased or when it is sold. During the time that it is held, its original cost is expensed periodically through the amortization entry, but there is no cash flow when this entry is recorded. Amortization does look like a source of cash in the indirect approach to preparing the cash flow statement; it is an add-back to the net income in this section. Appearances are deceiving, however, since the reason for adding back the amortization is to correct for the fact that amortization, which is imbedded in the net income number, does not affect cash flows and must therefore be removed from net income in order to arrive at cash flow from operations.

5-9   a) Financing
      b) Investing
      c) Operating
      d) Financing
      e) Investing
      f) Financing
      g) Investing
      h) While the collection of an individual receivable would be excluded, the change in total receivables would be included in the cash flow from operations under the indirect method
      i) Does not appear on the cash flow statement because the declaration of dividends has no impact on the cash position of a company until the dividends are paid
      j) Investing

5-11 The total cash flows from investing activities are often negative as companies expand. The cash outflow indicates the company is acquiring new capital assets (land, plant, equipment, long-term investments, etc.). These cash outflows can continue as long as a company has cash or can arrange new financing. A positive cash flow from investing, however, would indicate a company is selling capital assets. Such assets can only be sold once, so there is a limit to the amount of cash inflow that can be produced.

APPLYING YOUR KNOWLEDGE SOLUTIONS

5-13 A high sales growth rate can cause a company a cash flow problem if there is a significant lead/lag relationship between the expenditure of costs and the receipt of revenues. The high growth rate causes the company to purchase larger quantities of inventories and this incurs a significant amount of cost. If there is a lag between purchase and sale, and then sale and collection, these costs do not get covered by corresponding revenues in the short run. The high growth rate exacerbates any lead/lag relationship that already exists. Depending on the characteristics of inventory purchase and the lead/lag relationship there is, in fact, a growth rate beyond which a company will perpetually be in need of infusions of cash. Most companies cannot sustain these high growth rates for long, but during the early high growth years of many startup companies the demand for cash is great.

5-15 Interest cash flows are classified as operating activities on the cash flow statement because interest is deducted in the calculation of net income, and net income is used to derive cash flows from operations. Conceptually, this is not appropriate because interest represents payments to debtholders, which is a financing activity.

5-17

a) Amortization expense
   License (A)

Amortization expense	12,500	No effect on cash
License (A)	12,500	Operating activities: add back the $12,500 because it has been deducted from net income.

b) Cash   90,000

b)	Cash	90,000	Increases cash: $90,000
	Accumulated amort'n	95,000	Operating activities: deduct gain of $20,000
	Asset	165,000	Investing activities: report cash inflow of $90,000
	Gain on sale of asset	20,000	
c)	Asset	250,000	Decreases cash: $50,000
	Cash	50,000	Investing activities: report cash outflow of $50,000
	Notes payable	200,000	
d)	Interest expense	70,000	Decreases cash: $70,000 (reflected in operating activities through net income)
	Cash	70,000	
e)	Income tax expense	95,000	Decreases cash: $80,000
	Cash	80,000	Operating activities: as taxes payable increased from the prior year, add the $15,000 difference
	Taxes payable	15,000	

5-19 a) and b)

Trans. No.	Cash	Activity	Other Current Assets	Noncurrent Assets	Current Liabilities	Noncurrent Liabilities	Shareholders' Equity
1	+150,000	Financing					+150,000
2	-70,000	Investing		+110,000			+40,000
3	+2,000	Operating			+2,000		
4	+37,500	Operating			+37,500		
5			+210,000		+210,000		
6			-10,000		-10,000		
7	+360,000	Operating	+90,000				+450,000
8	-215,000	Operating			-215,000		
9	+9,000	Investing		-10,000			-1,000
10	-900	Investing	+900				
11	-200,000	Investing		+200,000			
12	-2,500	Operating					-2,500
13	-10,000	Operating			-37,500		+27,500
14	+100,000	Financing				+100,000	
15	+15,000	Investing	+20,000	-30,000			+5,000
16	-5,500	Operating		-20,000	-5,500		
17							
18	-2,000	Financing			+5,000		-20,000
19	-15,000	Investing		+15,000			-7,000
20	-45,000	Operating					-45,000

5-21 Cash Flow from Operations

	I	II	III
Net Income (loss)	104,000	115,000	106,000
Add:			
Amortization expense	25,000	35,000	40,000
Loss on sale		8,000	
Decrease in inventories			12,000
Decrease in accounts receivable	8,000		7,000
Increase in interest payable	2,000	4,000	
Increase in accounts payable	6,000		
Less:			
Gain on sale	10,000		6,000
Increase in inventories	12,000	10,000	
Increase in accounts receivable		8,000	
Decrease in interest payable			1,000
Decrease in accounts payable		6,000	3,000
Cash Flow from Operations	123,000	138,000	155,000

5-23   **a)**

Matrix Incorporated
Statement of Income and Retained Earnings
For the year ended December 31, 2004

Sales Revenues		$350,000
Expenses:		
Cost of Goods sold	$275,500	
Amortization Expense	10,000	
Rent Expense	12,000	
Interest Expense	15,000	
Salary Expense	24,000	
		336,500
Net Income		13,500
Retained Earnings		
December 31, 2003		2,500
Retained Earnings		
December 31, 2004		$16,000

b)

Matrix Incorporated
Balance Sheet
December 31, 2004

Assets:	
Cash	$ 2,900
Accounts receivable	12,500
Prepaid rent	6,000
Inventories	18,900
Total current assets	40,300
Property, plant and equipment	160,000
Accumulated amortization	(45,500)
Net property, plant and equipment	114,500
Total Assets	$154,800

Liabilities

Accounts payable	$ 13,800
Interest payable	9,000
Salaries payable	6,000
Current liabilities	28,800
Bonds payable	10,000
Total liabilities	38,800

Shareholders' Equity

Common shares	100,000
Retained earnings	16,000
Total shareholders' equity	116,000
Total liabilities and shareholders' equity	$154,800

c)

Matrix Incorporated
Cash Flow Statement
For the year ended December 31, 2004

Operations	
Net income	$13,500
Add back Amortization	10,000
Increase in Accounts Receivable	(2,500)
Increase in Prepaid Rent	(6,000)
Decrease in Notes Receivable	5,000[1]
Decrease in Inventories	1,600
Increase in Accounts Payable	8,800
Increase in Interest Payable	9,000
Decrease in Salaries Payable	(12,000)
Cash flow from operations	27,400
Investing	
Cash flow from investing	0
Financing	
Repayment of Bonds	(40,000)
Cash flow from financing	(40,000)
Net Change in Cash	($12,600)

[1] This would have been classified as an investing activity if it had not arisen as a result of the sale of inventory.

A-Cash

	√	15,500			
Operations:					
Net income	(1)	13,500	2,500	(3)	Incr. In Acc. Rec.
Amortization	(2)	10,000	6,000	(6)	Incr. In Prepd. Rt.
Decr. In Inv.	(4)	1,600	12,000	(8)	Decr. In Sal. Pay.
Decr. in Note Rec	(5)		5,000		
Incr. In Acc. Pay	(7)	8,800			
Incr. In Int. Pay.	(9)	9,000			
Financing:					
			40,000	(10)	Repmt. of Debt
	√	2,900			

A-Accounts Receivable			A-Inventories	
√	10,000		√ 20,500	
(3)	2,500			1,600 (4)
√	12,500		√ 18,900	

A-Trade Notes Receivable

√	5,000		
		5,000	(5)
√	0		

A-Prepaid Rent

√	0		
(6)	6,000		
√	6,000		

A-PP&E

√	160,000		
√	160,000		

XA-Accumulated Amortization

		35,500	√
		10,000	(2)
		45,500	√

L-Accounts Payable

		5,000	√
		8,800	(7)
		13,800	√

L-Salaries Payable

		18,000	√
(8)	12,000		
		6,000	√

L-Interest Payable

		0	√
		9,000	(9)
		9,000	√

L-Bonds Payable

		50,000	√
(10)	40,000		
		10,000	√

SE-Retained Earnings

		2,500	√
		13,500	(1)
		16,000	√

SE-Common Shares

		100,000	√
		100,000	√

Pentagon Company
Cash Flow Statement
Year ended December 31, 2004

Operations

Net Income	$ 35,000	
Add back amortization	25,000	
Decrease in accounts receivable	14,000	
Increase in inventories	(20,000)	
Decrease in prepaid expenses	10,000	
Decrease in accounts payable	(77,000)	
Decrease in wages payable	(20,000)	
Cash flow from operations		$(33,000)

Investing

Purchase of property, plant and equipment	(25,000)	
Cash flow from investing		(25,000)

Financing

Issue of bonds	25,000	
Issue of common shares	25,000	
Cash flow from financing		50,000

Net Change in cash	(8,000)
Cash position beginning of year	
	28,000
Cash position end of year	$20,000

5-27 a)

Pharmex Pharmaceutical Company
Statement of Income and Retained Earnings
Year ended December 31, 2004

Sales	$1,052,000
Gain on sale of property, plant, and equipment	15,000
	1,067,000
Less: Cost of goods sold	878,000
Amortization expense	75,000
Interest expense	60,000
Rent expense	85,000
Total expenses	1,098,000
Net income (Loss)	(31,000)
Retained Earnings December 31, 2003	386,000
Dividends	(20,000)
Retained Earnings December 31, 2004	$335,000

b)

Pharmex Pharmaceutical Company
Cash Flow Statement
Year ended December 31, 2004

Operations:		
Net income (Loss)	($31,000)	
Add: Amortization	75,000	
Deduct: Gain on sale of property, plant, and equipment	(15,000)	
Increase in accounts receivable	(50,000)	
Increase in inventories	(29,000)	
Decrease in accounts payable	(15,000)	
Cash flow from Operations		$(65,000)
Investing Activities:		
Purchase of machinery	(135,000)	
Proceeds on sale of machinery	115,000	
Cash flow from Investing		(20,000)

Financing Activities

Bonds Issued	25,000	
Shares Issued	50,000	
Dividends paid	(20,000)	
Cash flow from Financing		55,000
Net change in cash		$(30,000)
Beginning cash balance		80,000
Ending cash balance		$50,000

T-Account Worksheet

A-Cash

√	80,000				
Operations:					
Amortization (2)	75,000	31,000	(1)	Net Loss.	
		15,000	(3)	Gain on sale of PP&E	
		50,000	(4)	Inc. in A/R	
		29,000	(5)	Inc. in Inv.	
		15,000	(7)	Dec. in A/P	
Investing:					
Proceeds from sale of machinery (3)	115,000	135,000	(6)	Acquisition of machinery	
Financing:					
Proceeds from: Issuance of bonds (8)	25,000	20,000	(10)	Dividends paid	
Issuance of stocks (9)	50,000				
√	50,000				

A-Inventory			A-Accounts Receivable	
√ 296,000			√ 185,000	
(5) 29,000			(4) 50,000	
√ 325,000			√ 235,000	

A-Machinery			XA-Accumulated Amortization	
√ 545,000				122,500 √
(6) 135,000	125,000 (3)		(3) 25,000	75,000 (2)
√ 555,000				172,500 √

L-Accounts Payable			L-Bonds Payable	
	97,500 √			150,000 √
(7) 15,000				25,000 (8)
	82,500 √			175,000 √

SE-Common Shares			SE-Retained Earnings	
	350,000 √			386,000 √
	50,000 (9)		(1) 31,000	
			(2) 20,000	
	400,000 √			335,000 √

5-29 a)

Cash generated from operations:	
Net income	$388,900
Adjustments:	
Amortization expense	67,000
Amortization of patent	3,800
Gain on sale of equipment	(5,000)
Increase in accounts receivable	(13,000)

Decrease in inventory 7,000
Increase in accounts payable 3,500
Decrease in wages payable (1,300)
Increase in income taxes payable 3,100
Cash generated from operations $454,000

Supporting calculations:
  Amortization of patent: $3800 = $31,200 - $27,400
  Gain on sale of equipment: $5,000 = $22,000 - $17,000

b)

Cash flow from investing activities:
  Purchase of patent $(31,200)
  Purchase of equipment (516,000)
  Proceeds on sale of equipment 22,000
  Cash used in investing $(525,200)

Supporting calculations:
Purchase of equipment: $516,000 = $465,000 + $51,000

c)

Cash flow from financing activities:
  Cash dividends paid $(52,000)
  Purchase of common shares (44,000)
  Proceeds from sale of bonds 100,000
  Cash generated by financing $ 4,000

d)

Downsview Company
Cash Flow Statement
Year ended December 31, 2004

<u>Operations</u>		
Net Income	$388,900	
Add: amortization of plant & equip.	67,000	
amortization of patent	3,800	
Gain on sale of equipment	(5,000)	
Increase in taxes payable	3,100	
Increase in accounts receivable	(13,000)	
Decrease in inventories	7,000	
Increase in accounts payable	3,500	
Decrease in wages payable	<u>(1,300)</u>	
Cash Flow from operations		$454,000
<u>Investing</u>		
Purchase of patent	$(31,200)	
Purchase of plant and equipment	(516,000)	
Sale of equipment	<u>22,000</u>	
Cash flow from investing		(525,200)
<u>Financing</u>		
Issue of bonds	$100,000	
Redemption of common shares	(44,000)	
Dividends	<u>(52,000)</u>	
Cash flow from financing		<u>4,000</u>
Net Change in cash		$(67,200)
Beginning cash balance		<u>261,800</u>
Ending cash balance		<u>$194,600</u>

USER PERSPECTIVE SOLUTIONS

5-31 The operations section includes the cash flows that result directly from the sale of goods and services to customers. This is the company's core reason for being in business. This cash flow is useful in predicting future cash flows as the company's core business is likely to continue from one year to the next. Cash flows from financing and investing, however, may not appear at similar levels each year, so these cash flows are not as useful in predicting future cash flows.

Also, because the cash inflows from investing and financing are limited by the willingness of lenders and investors to support the company, a user looks for positive cash flow from operations to ensure that it is sufficient over the long term to pay for the continuing investing and financing activities.

The cash flow from operations section starts with the net income figure, and by comparing net income to cash flow from operations, the user can determine the significance of the company's lead/lag relationships. Large differences between net income and cash flow signal the importance to the company in monitoring credit relationships with customers and suppliers and monitoring the company's ability to sell inventory quickly. The analysis of changes in non-cash working capital accounts can indicate specific problems with accounts receivable, accounts payable, or inventory policies. For example, a cash outflow from an increase in accounts receivable may signal a problem with collectibility from customers. This may require the company to review credit-granting policies or to offer incentives to customers for early payment.

5-33 The stock analyst attempts to assess and value the productive capabilities of a company. Those productive capabilities are played out over long periods of time and hence the income statement is likely to be a better source of information in trying to predict future results. The analyst cannot, however, ignore the cash flow statement as it provides useful information about the ability of the company to meet is cash flow and liquidity needs. If the company is unsuccessful in managing its cash position in the short run, it may not make it to the long run to capture the value that is represented in its forecasted earnings. Yet, if you had to decide which statement would likely be more useful, you would conclude that the income statement is more useful to the analyst.

5-35 In general, lenders should be quite satisfied with the classification of cash flows into the three categories of operating, investing, and financing activities. These activities represent the sources (financing) and uses (investing) of cash, in addition to the cash generated as a result of investment in business activities (operating). However, the classification of interest as an operating activity is inappropriate in the sense that interest represents a return paid to lenders, and is thus related to financing rather than to the revenue-generating activities of the business.

5-37 a) Sources of cash flow for Green Company:

	Dollar Amount	**% of Total**
Operating activities	$ 720,000	33.96%
Sale of operating assets	400,000	18.87%
Issuance of common shares	1,000,000	47.17%
Total	$2,120,000	100.00%

Uses of cash flow for Green Company:

	Dollar Amount	% of Total
Purchase of operating assets	$1,200,000	43.64%
Retirement of bonds	1,300,000	47.27%
Dividends paid	250,000	9.09%
Total	$2,750,000	100.00%

One of the reconciling items between net income and cash provided by operations is a deduction of $120,000 for the change in current assets other than cash. Because the amount is deducted, it means that current assets increased. An increase in current assets would be consistent with an increase in sales. As sales increase, so would accounts receivable (if sales are made on credit) and inventory levels.

b) Green Company appears to have reduced its financial risk during 2004. A total of $1,300,000 of bonds were retired and $1,000,000 of additional shares were issued. The decrease in debt will decrease requirements to repay interest and principal, which gives Green Company more flexibility in times of tight cash flow.

c) The question does not provide information on the total asset base, so we do not know how large an investment in capital assets already exists. However, $1,200,000 of new operating assets were purchased and $400,000 were sold, resulting in a net investment of $800,000. This net investment is substantially more than the $230,000 of amortization expense charged on existing assets in 2004. By examining total investment in capital assets and accumulated amortization, a clearer picture of the rate of expansion that occurred in 2004 can be obtained. It would also be appropriate to examine the notes to see if some portion of the assets acquired had previously been leased. If the assets previously had been leased, a cost savings may be realized through ownership, but there may have been no change in total productive capacity.

d) Green Company reduced its net financing by $300,000 and experienced an overall decrease in cash of $630,000. This indicates that additional financing is required if Green expects to continue expanding and to continue dividend payments of $250,000.

READING AND INTERPRETING PUBLISHED FINANCIAL STATEMENTS SOLUTIONS

5-39 a) Sources of cash

	Dollar Amount	% of Total
Cash from operations	$20,717,339	49.0
Increase in utilitization of bank credit facilities	6,300,056	14.9
Issuance of shares	8,931,068	21.1
Decrease in accounts receivable	337,473	0.8
Increase in accounts payable	3,181,290	7.5
Disposition of property, plant and equipment	2,671,680	6.4
Disposition of marketable securities	118,699	0.3
Payment from Laird resources	6,862	0.01
	$42,264,467	100.0

b) Uses of cash

	Dollar Amount	% of Total
Purchase of property, plant and equipment	$39,764,985	83.1
Repurchase of common shares	7,815,836	16.3
Repayment of capital leases	79,287	0.2
Share purchase loans	73,250	0.2
Purchase of marketable securities	22,233	0.05
Issue of special warrants	65,050	0.15
	$47,820,641	100.0

c) Accounts receivable decreased $2,726,734; prepaid expenses and deposits decreased $4,733,661; inventories decreased $45,403; accounts payable and accrued liabilities decreased $2,047,511; corporate taxes payable decreased $54,298.

d) The overall cash flow of Purcell Energy Ltd. improved in 2001. There was still an overall decrease in cash of $5,685, but this was an improvement over the 2000 decrease of $9,972. This was the result of the decline in net income, from $8,225,838 in

2000 to $7,413,678 in 2001. The decline in earnings was offset when cash flows were considered, as the non-cash expenses in the income statement increased from $9,663,8190 in 2000 to $13,303,681 in 2001. Thus the cash flow from operations improved, from $17,889,657 in 2000 to $20,717,337 in 2001. The company also generated $6,300,056 of cash in 2001 by increasing bank credit facilities, versus $10,989,434 in 2001. These two major sources of cash (operations and increased bank credit facilities) were primarily used to fund the $39,764,985 purchases of property, plant and equipment. In addition, there were significant cash swings related to changes in the company's capital structure, although these net to a smaller overall change. $7,880,886 was spent to repurchase common shares and $8,931,068 raised through the issues of common shares and special warrants.

5-41 (All amounts in thousands of U.S. dollars)

a) Bema Gold has been operating at a loss in each of the three years, with 2000 representing the largest loss of $51,139. Losses were substantially reduced in 2001 to about one fifth of 2000 but were still almost three times greater than the 1999 results.

Many of the items that contributed to the losses did not affect cash. In 2000, losses were largely driven by a writedown in mineral properties of $22.6 million, the writedown in investments of $11.8 million, and investment losses of $9.3 million as Bema Gold appeared to be 'cleaning up' its balance sheet. In 2001, Bema recorded a modest investment gain of $554,000, but wrote down its inventory by $2.2 million.

Cash flows from operations were $6.3 million in 1999, sharply reduced from $666,000 in 2000 under the weight of the writedowns and further reduced to ($138,000) in 2001 with the writedown of inventory.

In each of the three years, Bema Gold has generated extra cash by issuing shares and warrants. In 1999, there was $3.6 million in new issues, declining to $3 million in 2000, increasing to $4.6 million in 2001.

In each of the three years, Bema Gold has been using cash to explore and develop new mines. Investment in Refugio mine ($4 million in each of 1999 and 2000) was largely completed in 2000, while a major new development effort was undertaken at the Julietta site (expenditures of $18.7 million in 2000 and $20 million in 2001). Both exploration and development are essential to Bema's long-term profitability

In 1999, loan repayments exceeded new borrowings as the Refugio loan was paid down. This $6 million repayment in 1999 and 2000 increased to $8 million in 2001. In 2000, Bema Gold borrowed $25.4 million under a new Julietta project loan and additional convertible loans. In 2001, they borrowed an additional $21.2 million for the Julietta project. Over the three years, the company has swung from equity as a major source of financing to debt.

b) The following additional information would be required: the current and expected future state of the mining industry; specific information on the Refugio mine and the feasibility of the Julietta site; when the company expects to make a profit; number of shares issued; and the current level of debt.

Other answers are possible.

5-43 (All amounts in thousands)

a) AT Plastics recorded a small loss of $2,494 in 1999 and much larger losses of $25,708 and $30,241 in 2000 and 2001. While its cash flow from operations was positive in 1999, in the past two years the cash flow from operations has been increasingly negative. Thus, the company has not generated sufficient cash to cover investing and financing activities.

In all three years the company has made principal repayments on long-term debt with an extremely large payment of $66,780 in 2001. The cash for the repayment came from three sources: issue of common shares, $32,312; issue of new long-term debt, $11,981; and proceeds from the sale of assets (Wire and Cable business, Packaging business, and other assets), $53,596.

The company has issued new shares in each of the last three years, but the last dividend payment was made in 1999.

The company has continued to purchase capital assets over the three years, reducing from $10,816 in 1999 to $7,236 in 2001. So the company appears to be maintaining some of its operations. But the sale of the Wire and Cable and Packaging businesses in 2001 is troubling. This generated cash to meet the debt repayment requirements, but will not be a recurring cash flow. The company appears to be downsizing its operations, which may further reduce cash flow from operations in the future.

b) The items that would require more investigation or further explanation would be: the reason for the large loss in 2001 (loss in 2000 was due to writedown of assets of discontinued operations); the reasons for the sale of Wire and Cable and Packaging businesses; the company's future needs for capital assets; the company's current debt load; and the company's ratio of debt to equity. Other answers are possible.

c) As noted in a), while there was a large loss in 2001, and cash flow from operations was marginal (but negative), the company ended 2001 with an overall increase in cash of $18,544 due to cash inflow of $32,312 from share issues, new long-term debt of $11,981, and cash proceeds of $53,596 from the sale of the Wire and Cable and Packaging businesses, and other assets. These cash inflows were sufficient to cover the $66,780 required for long-term debt repayments and $8,176 for capital purchases, and still leave an overall cash increase.

d) The cash payments for interest and income taxes are buried in the operating section of the cash flow statement. By identifying the cash paid for interest, it is possible to compare this to the amount of debt on the balance sheet to estimate the company's overall interest rate and assess this for reasonableness. This would be of interest to shareholders to determine the cost of capital financing and consider whether cheaper sources may be found. It also assists the company's lenders to ensure that interest payments on loans are kept up to date. A company that is having problems meeting interest payments will face more significant problems when principal payments on loans become due.

By identifying the cash paid for income taxes and comparing to income tax expense on the income statement, this will assist in identifying whether the company is up to date on payments required for taxing authorities. This would be of interest to all financial statement users: shareholders, lenders, and the tax authority itself. Tax authorities usually impose stiff penalties for non-payment and have sweeping powers to enforce payment, so a company that falls behind in these payments can face harsh consequences.

BEYOND THE BOOK SOLUTIONS

5-45 Answers to this question will depend on the company selected.

CHAPTER 6

Cash, Temporary Investments, and Accounts and Notes Receivable

ASSESSING YOUR RECALL SOLUTIONS

6-1 **Cash**:
Probable Future Value – The probable future value in cash is the ability of the cash to be exchanged for goods and services in the future.
Ownership – Ownership is evidenced by possession of currency and by the right to control bank accounts.

Temporary Investments:
Probable Future Value - The probable future value in temporary investments is the cash payments that will be received from the investments in the future. These payments take the form of dividends in the case of shares and interest in the case of debt as well as the ultimate sales price of the securities when they are sold.
Ownership – Ownership is evidenced by share or debt certificates, although sometimes these documents are not distributed to the owners but a record is kept by the brokerage house that handles the investments for the company.

Accounts Receivable:
Probable Future Value – The probable future value in accounts receivable is that they represent the right to receive cash at some (usually fixed) date in the future. The cash, in turn, has value in the ability to be exchanged for goods and services in the future.
Ownership – Ownership is evidenced by contracts either written or implied between the buyer and the seller. Invoices and

shipping documents usually provide the necessary evidence of proof that a receivable exists.

Notes Receivable:
Probable Future Value – The probable future value in notes receivable is that they represent the right to receive cash, either upon demand or at some fixed date in the future. The cash, in turn, has value in the ability to be exchanged for goods and services in the future.
Ownership – Ownership is evidenced by a promissory note or written contract between the maker and the payee.

6-3 Purchasing power risk is present for cash because when cash is held during periods of inflation the purchasing power of the dollar decreases. For example, if $100 is held in cash during a year of a price increase of 10% the $100 will buy 10% fewer goods and services at the end of the year, than at the beginning. Inventory, on the other hand, is not fixed in terms of the number of dollars that it represents. The value of the inventory can fluctuate with changing prices. If $100 worth of inventory was held during a year in which prices increased 10% it is possible that the price of the inventory could be raised to $110 to compensate. There may be supply and demand reasons why the price of inventory could not be raised to the full $110. If this is so then the inventory may be subject to some purchasing power risk but not to the same degree as cash.

6-5 At the end of every account period the accountant evaluates the cost and the current market value of the temporary investments portfolio. The book value of the portfolio at the end of the period must be the lower of cost and market value. After this determination is made, the carrying value of the portfolio (its cost less the current value in the valuation allowance account) is adjusted upwards or downwards to reflect the proper value at the end of the period. The adjustment is reported as an unrealized loss if the value of the portfolio is written down and an unrealized recovery if the value is written up.

6-7 The direct write-off method recognizes bad debt expense (loss) in the period in which the receivable is determined to be unrecoverable, not necessarily in the period in which the original sale was made. This creates a matching problem. The allowance method estimates and records the bad debt expense in the period of the original sale. This method provides a proper matching of the revenues and expenses (bad debt expense) from the sale and is the method that is most consistent with GAAP. The direct write-off method can be used if the results of applying it are not materially different from the results of applying the allowance method.

6-9 Two ratios that measure liquidity are the current ratio and the quick ratio. Both compare current assets to current liabilities, with the current ratio comparing total current assets and the quick ratio comparing total current assets less inventories and prepaid expenses. Both provide information on the ability of the company to pay its current liabilities, with the quick ratio providing more conservative information.

APPLYING YOUR KNOWLEDGE SOLUTIONS

6-11 a)

William's Carpet Company
Bank Reconciliation
March 31, 2xxx

Balance per bank statement		$54,622
Add: Outstanding deposit		10,200
		$64,822
Less: Outstanding cheques		(2,806)
Adjusted cash balance		$62,016
Balance per general ledger		$59,304
Add: Collection of note receivable		3,500
		62,804
Less: July service charge	18	
NSF cheque	70	
Loan payment	700	(788)
Adjusted cash balance		$62,016

b) At July 31, William's actually has $62,016 in its account.

c)	SE-Bank service charges	18	
	A-Cash		18
	A-Cash	3,500	
	A-Note receivable		3,500
	A-Accounts receivable	70	
	A-Cash		70
	L-Loan payable	700	
	A-Cash		700

6-13

Grace Ho
Bank Reconciliation

Balance per bank statement		$1,563
Less: Outstanding cheques		310
Adjusted cash balance		$ 1,253
Balance per cheque book		$ 1,243
Add: automatic deposit		50
		1,293
Less: error in recording cheque	$ 9	
NSF cheque	25	34
		1,259
Less: service charge ($1,259 - $1,253)		6
Adjusted cash balance		$1,253

6-15 a)

Income from operations	$45,000
Add: dividend income	900[1]
Deduct: unrealized loss on temporary investments	(1,500)
Net income	$44,400

[1](100 x $2) + (200 x $3.50) = $900

b) Return on investments = $900 / $10,500 = 8.57%
Duggan Company did not attain its goal of attaining a 10% annual return on its investments.

6-17 a)

Dec 31, 20x1	$410,000
20x2	480,000
20x3	480,000
20x4	530,000

b)

Dec 31, 20x1	SE-Unrealized loss on valuation of temporary investments	40,000	
	XA-Valuation allowance for temporary Investments		40,000
Dec 31, 20x2	XA-Valuation allowance for temporary investments	20,000	
	SE-Recovery of unrealized loss on valuation of temporary investments		20,000
Dec 31, 20x3	XA-Valuation allowance for temporary investments	20,000	
	SE-Recovery of unrealized loss on valuation of temporary investments		20,000
Dec 31, 20x4	SE-Unrealized loss on valuation of temporary investments	10,000	
	XA-Valuation allowance for temporary investments		10,000

6-19 a)

Income from operations	$640,000	
Add: dividend income	6,500[1]	
Deduct: unrealized loss on temporary investments	(500)	
Net Income	$646,000	

[1] (500 x $6) + (500 x $2) + (500 x $5) = $6,500

b) Return on investments = $6,500 / $56,500 = 11.5%
Upper Company did not attain its goal of attaining a 12% annual return on its investments.

6-21 a)

Selling Price	$50,000
Add: Loss on Sale	5,650
Cost Price	$55,650

Journal Entry for Sales

A-Cash	50,000	
SE-Loss on Sale of temporary investments	5,650	
A-Temporary investments		55,650

b)

Temporary Investments:

Ending Balance (at cost)	$313,000
Less: Purchases during 20x4	85,000
	228,000
Add: Sales during 20x4	55,650
Opening Balance (at cost)	$283,650

c) Valuation Allowance for Temporary

Ending Balance (20x4)	$13,000
Less: Unrealized loss on valuation	3,850
Beginning balance	$9,150

6-23 a)

A-Accounts receivable	820,000	
SE-Sales		820,000
A-Cash	790,000	
A-Accounts receivable		790,000
XA-Allowance for doubtful accounts	5,000	
A-Accounts receivable		5,000
SE-Bad debts expense	8,200	
XA-Allowance for doubtful accounts		8,200

b) Accounts receivable, December 31, 20x4 $145,000
    ($120,000+820,000-790,000-5,000)
     Less: Allowance for doubtful accounts   (7,200)
       Accounts receivable, net $137,800

6-25 a)

SE-Bad debt expense   6,930
   XA-Allowance for doubtful accounts   6,930
   ($1,540,000 x0.6x0.0075 = $6,930)

b)

Allowance for doubtful accounts

		3,300	0.5%x0.60x
Write off 2004	2,800		$1,100,000
		500	Balance 2004
Write off 2005	4,700	6,930	2005 allowance
		2,730	Balance 2005

c)

   Accounts receivable, December 31, 2005 $76,000
   Allowance for doubtful accounts   (2,730)
   Accounts receivable, net $73,270

6-27 a)

  June 1, A-Note receivable   36,000
  2004   SE-Sales   36,000

  Dec. 31, A-Interest receivable   2,310
  2004   SE-Interest revenue   2,310
        ($36,000 x .11 x 7/12 = $2,310)

Jan. 31   A-Cash   38,640
2005   A-Note receivable   36,000
                  A-Interest receivable   2,310
                  SE-Interest revenue   330
                  ($36,000 x .11 x 1/12 = $330)

b)

   Dec. 31, 2004 Balance sheet (Current assets)
   Note receivable $36,000
   Interest receivable   2,310

   Income statement for year ended Dec. 31, 2004
   Sales $36,000
   Interest revenue   2,310

6-29 a)

Current ratio $=$ $\dfrac{45,000 + 130,000 + 18,000 + 390,000 + 55,000}{85,000 + 37,000 + 45,000 + 10,000 + 115,000}$

$\qquad\qquad = \dfrac{638,000}{292,000}$

$\qquad\qquad = 2.18$

Quick ratio $=$ $\dfrac{638,000 - 390,000 - 55,000}{292,000}$

$\qquad\qquad = 0.66$

b) The company has been successful in achieving its desired results in terms of the current ratio, but it did not meet its target of 1.0 for the quick ratio. Also, the quick ratio has dropped dramatically from 1.2 last year to 0.66 this year.

c) The company could improve its current position through reducing its substantial investment in inventory, so long as the resulting effect on sales is not severe. Reducing the inventory levels would free up some cash, and thus enable the company to better meet its current obligations. In addition, Liquid Company could attempt to reduce its current levels of short-term liabilities, which would also improve its current position.

6-31

Smythe Company
Cash Flow Statement
Year ended December 31, 2004

Operating Activities:	
Net income	$ 1,635
Add back amortization	1,000
Increase in accounts receivable	(45)
Increase in inventory	(450)
Increase in accounts payable	150
Net cash provided by operating activities	2,290
Investing Activities:	
Purchase of property, plant and equipment	(2,200)
Increase in cash	$ 90
Cash position*, beginning of year	
Cash	$ 500
Temporary investments, net of allowance	450
	$ 950
Cash position, end of year	
Cash	$ 540
Temporary investments, net of allowance	500
	1,040
Increase in cash	$ 90

*NOTE: Recall that cash position in the Cash Flow Statement reflects "cash equivalents," which includes both cash and temporary investments.

USER PERSPECTIVE SOLUTIONS

6-33 A stock option plan that rewards managers for achieving a certain level of reported net income has the potential to influence management's assessment of the collectibility of its accounts receivable. For example, if management determines that the year-end balance of accounts receivable is collectible in full, then no bad debt expense is booked, and the reported net income is higher as a result.

6-35 As a shareholder I will be interested in the market value of temporary investments because this provides an indication of the cash that will be available when the investments are sold (likely within one year) and any gains/losses from the carrying value will affect net income.

   The cash flow information can assist in evaluating the company's liquidity and the potential for dividends. A measurement of net income that includes investment gains may better help predict future income and share price.

6-37 Bank reconciliations are important for the management of cash because they keep the company up-to-date in terms of recording all transactions that affect its cash balance. In doing so, the company can assess its need for cash, or perhaps plan short-term investments in order to earn a return on excess cash. Bank reconciliations are also a good internal control over cash because their basic function is to reconcile independent records of the same bank account.

6-39 **a)** and **b)**

	2004	2003	2002
Allowance for doubtful accounts	$128.9	$21.9	$118.0
Total accounts receivable	$1,598.7	$1,352.5	$1,162.8
% considered uncollectible	8.06%	1.62%	10.15%
Bad debt expense	$312.4	$271.5	$267
Sales	$12,661.8	$11,367.8	$10,420
Bad debt expense as a % of sales	2.47%	2.39%	2.56%

c) Although the actual number of write-offs in dollars has fluctuated during the three-year period, the highest percentage of accounts written off in relation to either accounts receivable or operating revenues was in 2002. It appears from the following analysis that Lowrate improved considerably in 2003 and is doing roughly the same in 2004:

	2004	2003	2002
Accounts written off / sales	2.45%	2.38%	2.85%
Accounts written off / accounts receivable	19.38%	19.98%	25.52%

d) Lowrate Communications records revenue and an account receivable when it bills its customers. Since customers are not liable for calls that were not made by the customers due to car phone theft, cloning, etc., Lowrate removes these charges from the customers' accounts and must reduce receivables. At the same time, the company must record a reduction in recorded revenue, reduce the allowance for doubtful accounts, or establish an expense account (bad debt). Another option would be to establish one or more separate expense accounts in which these losses are recorded to track them more closely. It is not readily apparent from the financial data presented how Lowrate handles this situation. However, if it is handled through the allowance for doubtful accounts, we would expect the amounts reported as bad debts, the allowance for doubtful accounts, and the amount actually written off to increase.

READING AND INTERPRETING PUBLISHED FINANCIAL STATEMENTS SOLUTIONS

6-41 Cash can include short-term marketable securities if the securities are held as a substitute for cash and as long as the investments are readily marketable. According to GAAP, the short-term investments must mature within 90 days from the balance sheet date in order to be classified as cash.

Mosaid's short-term marketable securities may not be included in cash as they may not be capable of prompt liquidation, or mature more than 90 days from the balance sheet date. If both conditions were met, they could be included in cash as a cash equivalents balance.

6-43 a) Percentage uncollectible in 2000 = $18/($404+18) = 4.27%
Percentage uncollectible in 2001 = $19/($300+19) = 5.96%

b) 2000 Accounts receivable turnover = $3,598 / $422 = 8.53
365/8.53 = 43 days

2001 Accounts receivable turnover = $4,377 / $319 = 13.72
365/13.72 = 27 days

c) Accounts receivable can be sold to other parties, who then collect from the customer. This allows the company selling accounts receivable to collect cash more quickly, although the cash received is less than the face value of the accounts receivable, as the purchaser will charge a fee. Selling accounts receivable on a limited recourse basis means that the purchaser of the accounts receivable assumes primary responsibility for collection and absorbs any credit losses.

6-45 a) 2001: $23,199,678/$1,593,984 = 14.56
365/14.56 = 25 days
2000: $22,716,926/$1,872,064 = 12.13
365/12.13 = 30 days

Big Rock is collecting its accounts receivable in a shorter time, 25 days in 2001, as compared to 2000 when it collected its accounts receivable on average every 30 days. Note that 2001 sales have increased 2% over 2000 levels, while the 2001 accounts receivable balance has actually decreased almost 15% from the prior year.

b) A-Accounts receivable   23,199,678
   SE-Sales   23,199,678

   A-Cash   23,477,758
    A-Accounts receivable   23,477,758
   ($1,872,064+23,199,678-1,593,984 = $23,477,758)

BEYOND THE BOOK SOLUTIONS

6-47 Answers to this question will depend on the company selected.

CHAPTER 7

Inventory

ASSESSING YOUR RECALL SOLUTIONS

7-1 Under GAAP, inventory is carried at the lower of cost and market. Market is most commonly either replacement cost or net realizable value. When the calculated cost figure is materially different from recent cost figures, companies should be applying the lower of cost and market valuation method.

7-3 Replacement cost is the price at which an item could be replaced in inventory. This price is sometimes referred to as an entry price since it describes the price at which units of inventory enter the company. Net realizable value is the selling price of an item less any costs necessary to complete and sell the item. This price is sometimes referred to as an exit price since it describes the price at which units exit the company.

7-5 The advantage of the perpetual system over the periodic system is that management has continuously updated information available concerning inventories and cost of goods sold. This is very important for inventory management purposes. The disadvantage is that perpetual systems are more costly to implement. Prior to the advent of low-cost computing power, perpetual systems were only used for low-volume, high unit cost types of inventories (such as in a car dealership). Another advantage of the perpetual system is that inventory shrinkage can be independently determined by combining the perpetual information with a physical count. An additional cost of the perpetual system is that the company also has to count its inventory periodically to verify shrinkage and to assess the integrity of the perpetual information.

The advantage of the periodic system is that it is less costly. However, management does not have updated information about inventory levels. It also has a difficult time determining the amount of inventory shrinkage. The cost of goods sold is determined by adding the purchases for the period to the beginning inventory and then subtracting the inventory cost determined from the physical count. It is assumed that any inventory that is not there to be counted has been sold.

7-7 For reporting purposes, management typically has an incentive to report the highest possible income, particularly if there is a management incentive program based on reported income. Therefore, management would probably like to report the lowest amount of cost of goods sold so as to produce the highest net income. This incentive is obviously at odds with the incentive for tax purposes.

For tax purposes, a company typically would like to choose the cost flow assumption that would result in the highest cost of goods sold since that would produce the lowest taxable income and the lowest amount of taxes paid. In Canada, the Canada Customs and Revenue Agency will not allow LIFO to be used for tax purposes. This narrows the choice of methods that companies can use to achieve a low taxable income. The actual choice of methods for tax purposes would depend on whether prices are increasing or decreasing and whether inventory levels are expected to remain stable, increase, or decrease. Expected future changes in tax rates might also have some influence on the decision.

The choice of inventory methods is constrained because a company cannot switch back and forth between inventory methods at will. The accounting characteristic, consistency, discourages companies from switching methods frequently and a company's auditors would object to frequent switches for reporting purposes.

7-9   The three main reasons that a company would need to estimate cost of goods sold or inventory would be: 1) the inventory has been destroyed or stolen and it is impossible to count; 2) the company wants to prepare monthly financial statements but does not want to incur the cost of counting the inventory; and 3) the company wants to have an estimate of the inventory it has before it begins the physical count so that it can determine whether goods have been lost or stolen.

APPLYING YOUR KNOWLEDGE SOLUTIONS

7-11 a) Weighted average

	Unit Cost	Total Cost
Aug. 14, 6,000 on hand	$18.50	$ 111,000
Purchases: 8,000	$18.00	144,000
4,000	$17.50	70,000
12,000	$16.00	192,000
6,000	$14.50	87,000
36,000		$604,000

Average cost = $604,000 / 36,000 = $16.77 per unit
Units sold = 36,000 - 10,000 = 26,000
Cost of goods sold = 26,000 x $16.77 = $436,020

b) FIFO
Units sold = 36,000 - 10,000 = 26,000
Cost of goods sold = (6,000 x $18.50) + (8,000 x $18.00) +
(4,000 x $17.50) + (8,000 x $16.00) = $453,000

c) LIFO
Units sold = 36,000 - 10,000 = 26,000
Cost of goods sold = (6,000 x $14.50) + (12,000 x $16.00)+
(4,000 x $17.50) + (4,000 x $18.00) = $421,000

d) Because unit costs of purchases have been declining, LIFO
produces the greatest net income for August and FIFO
produces the smallest net income for August. LIFO cost of
goods sold expense is smallest and FIFO cost of goods sold
expense is greatest.

e) LIFO results in the largest inventory balance at August 31, because the high cost purchases from last period and those made at the beginning of August are assigned to inventory. FIFO results in the smallest inventory balance at August 31 because the low cost purchases made at the end of August are assigned to inventory.

f) The value assigned to cost of goods sold expense plus the value assigned to ending inventory add up to the same $604,000, cost of goods available for sale, regardless of the inventory cost flow assumption chosen. Thus a higher value for net income (LIFO) caused by lower cost of goods sold expense will result in higher ending inventory value.

7-13 a) FIFO
Total units sold = 270
Cost of Goods sold = (60 x $4) + (200 x $5) + (10 x $6)
                   = $1,300
Gross profit = (100 x $9) + (170 x $10) - $1,300
             = $1,300

b) LIFO
Total units sold = 270
Cost of goods sold = (60 x $7) + (40 x $6) + (170 x $5)
                   = $1,510
Gross profit = (100 x $9) + (170 x $10) - $1,510
             = $1,090

c) LIFO provides the most conservative estimate of the carrying value of inventory because it assigns lower costs from earlier purchases to ending inventory. Because inventory is stated at a lower amount under LIFO, there is less risk of overstatement, and a more conservative value results. LIFO also provides the best estimate of the current cost of replacing the inventory because cost of goods sold under this method reflects the cost of more recent purchases. As a result, gross profit is more representative of true profits, after allowing for the replacement of goods sold at their current costs.

b) LIFO provides the most conservative estimate of reported income, provided that prices are rising. If prices are in fact falling, FIFO provides the most conservative estimate of reported income.

7-15 a) Acquisition cost

Year	Sales	Cost of goods sold	Gross margin
1	$115,000	$ 65,000[1]	$50,000
2	$175,000	$ 95,000[2]	$80,000
3	$253,000	$163,000[3]	$90,000
4	$225,000	$145,000[4]	$80,000
			$300,000

Cost of goods sold = Beginning inventory + purchases ending inventory (at acquisition)

$\sqrt{ }$[1] $140,000 - $75,000 = $65,000
$\sqrt{ }$[2] $75,000 + $100,000 - $80,000 = $95,000
$\sqrt{ }$[3] $80,000 + $155,000 - $72,000 = $163,000
$\sqrt{ }$[4] $72,000 + $104,000 - $31,000 = $145,000

b) Lower of cost and market

Year	Sales	Cost of goods sold	Gross margin
1	$115,000	$ 70,000[1]	$ 45,000
2	$175,000	$103,000[2]	$ 72,000
3	$253,000	$150,000[3]	$103,000
4	$225,000	$145,000[4]	$ 80,000
			$300,000

Cost of goods sold = Beginning inventory + purchases –
ending inventory (at LCM)

$\sqrt{}^1$ $140,000 - $70,000 = $70,000
$\sqrt{}^2$ $70,000 + $100,000 - $67,000 = $103,000
$\sqrt{}^3$ $67,000 + $155,000 - $72,000 = $150,000
$\sqrt{}^4$ $72,000 + $104,000 - $31,000 = $145,000

c) The gross margin is higher using the acquisition cost basis in year one because market value has fallen below cost. If cost is used as the basis of valuation, ending inventory is higher and cost of goods sold is lower than under the lower of cost and market basis.

In year two, the higher inventory value is carried forward as beginning inventory, so that cost of goods sold would initially be expected to be higher under the acquisition cost basis. However, the market value of ending inventory is again below cost, making cost of goods sold lower (and gross margin higher) under the acquisition basis.
In year three, the cost of ending inventory is below its market value, so that cost (rather than market) is used under both the acquisition cost and the lower of cost and market methods. Still, the gross margin is higher under the lower of cost and market basis because a lower value of inventory is carried forward from the prior year as beginning inventory.
In the final year, the gross margin is the same under both methods because the cost and market values of inventory are the same, and beginning inventory is also the same for both methods.

d) The total gross margin for the four-year period is $300,000 under both valuation methods. Over the period, the beginning inventory valuation, $0, and ending inventory valuation, $31,000, would be the same under both valuation methods. Thus an equal amount of purchase costs flowed into cost of goods sold under both methods, resulting in the same total gross margin.

7-17 a) For 20x1, prices went down because LIFO results in a higher inventory value than FIFO.

b) For 20x4, prices went up because FIFO results in a higher inventory value than LIFO.

b) (HINT: To answer this question, assume purchases in each of the four years were $500,000. Calculate the COGS for each of the four years under each method. Remember that ending inventory from the previous year is the beginning inventory of the current year. The lowest COGS will produce the highest net income.) In 20x1 and 20x2, LIFO shows the highest income as cost of goods sold will be lower than under the other two valuation methods. In 20x3, FIFO shows the highest income. In 20x4, the lower of FIFO cost and market shows the highest net income.

	LIFO		FIFO		Lower of FIFO Cost and Market	
	End. Inv.	COGS	End. Inv.	COGS	End. Inv.	COGS
20x1	$65,000	$435,000	$60,000	$440,000	$55,000	$445,000
20x2	135,000	430,000	125,000	435,000	120,000	435,000
20x3	150,000	485,000	143,000	482,000	130,000	490,000
20x4	110,000	540,000	125,000	518,000	125,000	505,000
		$1,890,000		$1,875,000		$1,875,000

d) LIFO shows the lowest income for the four years combined, as its total cost of good sold expense is higher by $15,000. This is because LIFO ending inventory value on the balance sheet is $15,000 less than under the other two valuation methods.

7-19 a)

Beginning inventory	$28,000
Purchases	94,000
Ending inventory	**(??)**

Cost of goods sold   64% of $140,000 $89,600
Therefore, ending inventory should be $32,400

b) Insurance claim = $32,400 - $9,600 = $22,800

c) The estimate of ending inventory might be inaccurate if current-year conditions caused the cost-to-sales ratio to differ significantly from the estimate of 64%. Additional factors resulting in a potential error include errors in the count of beginning inventory and errors in the sales amount.

7-21 a)
Inventory turnover
Stream Ltd. $470 / [($120 + $100) / 2] = 4.27
Competitor $900 / [($280 + $250) / 2] = 3.40

b)
Gross margin percentage
Stream Ltd. ($600 - $470) / $600 = 21.7%
Competitor ($1,250 - $900) / $1,250 = 28%

c) On the basis of inventory turnover, Stream is superior because it turns over its inventory more often.

d) On the basis of gross margin percentage, the competitor is superior.

e) Based on the information available, it is not possible to determine which company is managed better. It does, however, make sense that the company that has the higher gross margin percentage also experiences lower turnover. Thus, management of each company is based on the competitive strategies adopted. It appears that Stream is attempting to sell more goods at a lower price while the competitor earns higher margins on inventory that turns over less often.

USER PERSPECTIVE SOLUTIONS

7-23 As an auditor, you would be concerned about the potential misstatement of inventories at year end. In particular, you would confirm that the inventory exists through a sample count, test for obsolete or damaged goods, and ensure that the balance recorded represents the minimum realizable amount of the goods that will be sold in the following year. Misstatements in these amounts affect both the income statement through cost of goods sold and the balance sheet in terms of the goods on hand recorded as an asset at year end. For example, if inventory is overstated at year end, then cost of goods sold is understated and net income is overstated.

7-25 In comparing a Canadian and a Japanese company you would first want to make sure that there were not significant differences in the accounting principles used by the two companies. If there are significant differences, then the best adjustment would be to convert them to the same principles if enough information is supplied to do so. For many ratios, such as ROI, current, and quick ratio, etc., there is no need to convert from yen to dollars as the units of currency are cancelled in the calculation of the ratio. Common size statements could also be used without any adjustment. The only time you might want to convert would be if you wanted to make some direct comparisons of balance sheet or income figures as a direct comparison of sales.

7-27 As a lender, you would be concerned if the company switched from LIFO to FIFO because this could be a signal that the company would not otherwise meet the restrictive debt covenant, and its sole motivation for switching accounting methods is to remain within the covenant. The switch to FIFO would mean ending inventory is valued at recent (higher) purchase costs, increasing the current ratio. However, FIFO does result in a more accurate representation of the cost of inventory on hand, because it allocates more recent costs to inventory. LIFO, on the other hand, can understate the current ratio because, during a period of rising prices, inventory is composed of the oldest costs. If the company was in financial distress, you would be much more concerned about an accounting change from LIFO to FIFO, because this change is likely an attempt to satisfy the debt covenants and improve reported operating profits.

7-29 **a)** The estimated cost of Black Light's inventory on hand at the end of the first quarter of 2004 is $410,000, estimated using the gross profit method as follows:

Cost of goods sold:		
Beginning inventory		$ 250,000
Purchases		650,000
Goods available for sale		900,000
Sales during the first quarter	$700,000	
Less estimated gross profit		
($700,000 x 30%)	(210,000)	
Estimated cost of goods sold		(490,000)
Estimated inventory at end of		
first quarter		$ 410,000

b) The gross profit method works reasonably well for interim estimates of inventory on hand, but it is not accurate enough to use regularly in annual financial statements. Changes in underlying cost patterns and other changes could easily result in highly inaccurate dollar amounts being reported if only estimates were used in determining the balance in inventory over a longer period of time. Some companies use the gross profit method to estimate inventory on a regular basis, but sometime during the year, they will conduct a physical count to adjust the estimate to the actual inventory on hand.

c) The gross profit method will provide reliable results so long as cost patterns remain stable, and the selling price and mark-ups are predictable. In general, all factors affecting the gross profit percentage must remain more or less unchanged for this method to provide reliable results.

d) Conditions that might cause the gross profit method to provide unreliable results include:
1. Price changes that were not recorded or taken into account in determining the gross profit margin.
2. Special merchandise purchases that are sold at a different gross profit margin.
3. Losses of inventory due to damage.
4. Losses of inventory due to theft and other causes.
5. Errors in recording inventory sales or purchases.

The gross profit method of inventory estimation is relevant and timely, but it is not objective and accurate enough for complete reliance.

e) Based on the estimate of Black Light's inventory at the end of the first quarter, the company's inventory position appears to be high. It is more than 60% larger than the balance on hand at the beginning of the quarter and, at the level of sales in the first quarter, it is enough inventory for more than 80% of the next quarter's sales. It may be that Black Light's business is seasonal and the inventory is needed for higher seasonal sales in the second quarter.

READING AND INTERPRETING PUBLISHED FINANCIAL STATEMENTS SOLUTIONS

7-31 **a)** In 2001, the inventory turnover was 107 days, which equaled the 2000 ratio. This turnover rate means that inventory sells in just over three and one half months. Based on the product life of beer, this is probably reasonable. Note: ending inventory, rather than average inventory is used in the turnover ratio calculations as the 2000 beginning inventory is unknown.

	2001	**2000**
COGS Expense	$9,240,503	$9,154,929
Inventory	$2,701,872	$2,676,790
	= 3.42 times	= 3.42 times
	= 107 days	= 107 days

b) The fourth item is promotional goods and dispensing units. The dispensing units are likely sold but probably not as quickly as the alcoholic products. The promotional goods are probably not sold at all. This item represents approximately 15% of the total inventory in 2001 ($412,281 / $2,701,982). If the inventory turnover is recalculated for 2001 omitting the fourth item, the turnover rate increases:

$9,240,503 / [($2,701,982 – 412,281)] = 4.04
365 / 4.04 = 90 days

The number of days inventory is held decreases by 17 days. The inclusion of the fourth item does make a difference.

c) Big Rock records returnable bottles as part of inventory and amortizes them over their useful lives. Some alternative ways that it could account for these bottles are:
1. to expense them as they are purchased
2. to record them at cost then expense them when they are used

7-33 a) Inventory Turnover

	Ratio	Days
2001	$25,927 / $799 = 32.45	11.2
2000	$47,025 / $3,117 = 15.09	24.2

The inventory turnover rate has more than doubled in 2001, due to a 45% decline in cost of sales but an almost 75% decline in inventories.

b) Based on the rapid changes that occur in software, a higher turnover is preferred in order to avoid carrying obsolete inventories. Thus, the fact that Corel's turnover has improved in 2001 might indicate effective management. However, selling its entire stock in approximately 11 days, while minimizing obsolescence problems, may run the risk of the company having insufficient inventory to meet unexpected customer demand. The reduction in inventory in 2001 may not be caused by more efficient management, but rather be a reflection of the problems that resulted from the large decline in sales revenue in 2001.

7-35 a)

Inventory Turnover

	Based on total inventory	Based on finished goods
2001	$1,552,561 / $128,421 = 12.1	$1,552,561/$75,149 = 20.7
2000	$1,598,525 / $154,484 = 10.3	$1,598,525/$93,441 = 17.1

b) Inventory turnover based on finished goods is more useful for users because the turnover ratio relates cost of sales to goods on hand that are ready for sale. Since only finished goods are sold, raw materials and work in process bear no relationship to cost of sales, and might distort the ratio.

BEYOND THE BOOK SOLUTIONS

7-37 Answers to this question will depend on the company selected.

CHAPTER 8

Capital Assets—Tangible and Intangible

ASSESSING YOUR RECALL SOLUTIONS

8-1 When plant, property, and equipment is purchased the intent of management is to use these assets to produce a product or provide a service. The value to the company is, therefore, the value of the products or services that the assets provide as they are being used. This type of value is referred to as value-in-use. If, on the other hand, the plant, property, or equipment was purchased with the intent to resell, then the value of the assets to the company would be the price at which the company could sell the assets. This type of value would be value-in-sale.

8-3 The cost of a basket purchase is allocated to the items on the basis of their relative fair market values. If there were three items (A, B, and C) purchased for a total of $1,000 and the fair market values of the three items were $300 (A), $400 (B), and $500 (C) then the cost of the three items would be allocated as follows:

Percentage of Fair Market Value   Cost
A: $300 / $1,200 = 25.0%
B: $400 / $1,200 = 33.3%
C: $500 / $1,200 = 41.7%

Cost
25.0% x $1,000 = $250
33.3% x $1,000 = $333
41.7% x $1,000 = $417

8-5 The purpose of amortization is to allocate the cost of a long-term asset over the life of the asset using a rational and systematic method. By allocating the cost of the life of the asset, the expenses related to the asset are matched with the revenues that are produced by the use of the asset. GAAP allows any method of amortization as long as it is systematic and rational. Several methods are used most commonly to achieve this allocation. In theory, the costs could be allocated in one of four general ways: evenly over the life of the asset (the straight-line method), more in the early years of the life of an asset and less in later years (an accelerated method), less in the early years of the life of an asset and more in later years (a decelerated method), or some method based on the actual usage of the asset. In practice the straight-line and accelerated methods are used more frequently. The decelerated method is almost never used. A commonly used accelerated method is the declining balance method.

8-7 Residual value and years of useful life are used directly in the straight-line method. Residual value is subtracted from the original cost of the asset to determine the amortizable cost of the asset, i.e. the amount of the cost that is to be amortized over the life of the asset. The useful life is then used to determine the fraction of the amortizable cost that is to be allocated to each period.

     For the production method, the residual value is also subtracted from the original cost of the asset to determine the amortizable cost of the asset. The useful life is estimated as the number of units of use or output that the asset will produce. Next the amortizable cost per unit is calculated. Finally the year's amortization expense is calculated by multiplying the actual use or output of the asset times the cost per unit.

     The declining balance method does not explicitly incorporate the residual value in the calculation of amortization expense. It is used as a constraint in setting the amortization schedule. Under this method the amortization expense each period is the declining balance percentage multiplied by the remaining net balance in the asset account (cost – accumulated amortization). Residual value is used in the last portion of the amortization schedule so as to prevent the company from amortizing the asset to a value less than the residual value. This may mean that the company records less amortization than the calculation would indicate in the final year. Another possibility is that the company will not have taken enough amortization by the end of the useful life and the residual value is then used to determine how much amortization to take in the last year to ensure that the carrying value of the asset at the end of its useful life is exactly the residual value. The useful life of the asset is used to determine the declining balance percentage used to calculate the annual amortization expense.

8-9 Capital Cost Allowance is applied in a manner that is quite similar to accelerated amortization. The main difference is that the Canada Customs and Revenue Agency specifies the maximum rate that may be used. Similar to accelerated amortization, the rate is applied to the unamortized balance (called Unamortized Capital Cost). Another difference is that only one-half the normal amount of Capital Cost Allowance is allowed to be recorded in the year the asset is acquired. There are some other differences, such as the recording of disposal and the grouping of assets into "pools."

8-11 The general guideline in GAAP is that intangibles can be recorded in the books if they are purchased from outside parties. Therefore, goodwill is recorded only when one company buys another and pays more for the company than the fair market value of its identifiable net assets. Research and development is required to be expensed as incurred, except for certain developmental costs. The costs of developing a patent would primarily be classified as research and development costs and these would be expensed. It is possible to capitalize the legal costs of establishing the patent, but these are typically a trivial part of the patent's cost.

The rules for expensing the capitalized cost of intangibles are that the cost should be amortized over the useful life of the intangible. This means using the lesser of the useful economic life and the legal life of the asset (as in the case of a patent). When the useful life is indeterminate, GAAP requires the maximum assumed life of the intangible asset be 40 years. Goodwill is no longer required to be amortized, but should be written down if and when its value is impaired.

APPLYING YOUR KNOWLEDGE SOLUTIONS

8-13 a) Amount to be capitalized:

		Building	Equipment
Jan. 4	Received equipment		$95,000
Jan. 24	Transportation of equipment		2,400
Jan. 27	Architect's fees	$ 7,500	
May 9	Completion of building	250,000	
May 14	Installing equipment		2,000
June 7	Testing of equipment		1,000
		$257,500	$100,400

b) The cost of advertising for workers and the cost of the party should be treated as a current period expense. There were no necessary costs in getting the equipment ready for use.

c) If Cedar Homes had borrowed money to finance expansion of the facilities, interest could have been capitalized as part of the cost of the building during its construction, but prior to its use. The second option is for Cedar Homes to just expense the interest in the current period.

8-15 a) The value assigned to the press should be based on its historical cost of $440,000. The company appears to be a going-concern and not in danger of being forced to sell the asset. Because the company has owned the press for four years, the net carrying value should be $264,000 based on the purchase price ($440,000) and accumulated amortization [($440,000 / 10) x 4].

b) The $950,000 value should not be recorded. This amount represents the expected profit from owning and using an asset. As the asset is used, the cost of the asset should be recognized. It is not appropriate to recognize the expected profit from using the printing press at the time it is purchased or at any time during the period it is used.

c) The $600,000 amount should not be recorded. The current press is already four years old and may not have all of the capabilities of a new press. Thus, it is unlikely the current press is worth that amount. However, even it if were, the $440,000 historical cost should continue to be used as the basis of accountability. It represents the more conservative amount.

d) The estimated sale price should be considered if the company is not a going-concern or decides to sell the asset. However, since the estimated sale price of $310,000 is greater than the current carrying value of $264,000, the concept of conservatism would support leaving the carrying value at the amortized historical cost.

8-17 a) 1. Straight-line amortization
   Calculation: [($95,000 -$5,000) / 6] = $15,000 per year

2. Double-declining balance amortization
   Calculation:
   20x1 ($95,000) x [(1/6) x 2] = $31,667
   20x2 ($95,000 - $31,667) x [(1/6) x 2] = $21,111
   20x3 ($95,000 - $31,667 - $21,111) x [(1/6) x 2] = $14,074
   20x4 ($95,000 - $31,667 - $21,111 - $14,074) x [(1/6) x 2] = $9,383
   20x5 ($95,000 - $31,667 - $21,111 - $14,074 - $9,383) x [(1/6) x 2] = $6,255
   20x6 Book value = $95,000 - $31,667- $21,111- $14,074 - $9,383 - $6,255 = $12,510

Residual value	5,000
Amortization for 20x6	$7,510

Amortization

	20x1	20x2	20x3	20x4	20x5	20x6
Straight-line	$15,000	$15,000	$15,000	$15,000	$15,000	$15,000
Double-declining	$31,667	$21,111	$14,074	$ 9,383	$ 6,255	$ 7,510

b) Amortization expense:

	Straight-line	Double Declining Balance
1. Over 1st 3 years	$45,000	$66,852
2. Over all 6 years	$90,000	$90,000

Double declining balance method records higher amortization expense over the first three years, but total expense is the same under both methods.

8-19

Oct. 31, 20x3	A-Machine	125,000	
	A-Cash		125,000
Dec. 31, 20x3	SE-Amortization expense	2,000	
	XA-Acc. amortization		2,000

[($125,000 - $5,000) / 10 x 2/12]

Dec. 31, 20x6	SE-Amortization expense	9,600	
	XA-Acc. amortization		9,600

Calculation:

Accumulated amortization, Jan. 01, 20x6
= $2,000 + 2 x [($125,000 - $5,000) / 10] = $26,000

Net book value, Jan. 01, 20x6
= $125,000 - $26,000 = $99,000

New amortization expense
= ($99,000 - $3,000) / 10 = $9,600

Amortization expense, June 30, 20x8
= $9,600 x 6/12 = $4,800

Accumulated amortization, June 30, 20x8
= $26,000 + (2 x $9,600) + $4,800 = $50,000

Net book value, June 30, 20x8
= $125,000 - $50,000 = $75,000

June 30, 20x8

SE-Amortization expense	4,800	
XA-Acc. amortization		4,800
A-Cash	82,000	
XA-Accumulated amortization	50,000	
A-Machine		125,000
SE-Gain on sale of machine		7,000

8-21 a) and b)

March 31, 20x4	SE-Amortization expense	525	
	XA-Accumulated amort.		525
	A-Machine (new)	42,600	
	XA-Accumulated amort.	5,775	
	A-Machine (old)		22,000
	A-Cash		20,375
	L-Note payable		6,000
March 31, 20x9	XA-Accumulated amort.	33,000	
	SE-Loss due to write-off of machine	9,600	
	A-Machine		42,600

Calculations:

Old machine

Amortization until date of trade-in: $525 = [($22,000 - $1,000) / 10] \times 3/12$

Accumulated amortization = $5,775= [($22,000 - $1,000) / 10] \times 6/12 + 2 \times [($22,000 - $1,000) / 10] + 525

New machine

Purchase price of machine: $42,600 = $20,375 + $6,000 + ($22,000 - $5,775)$

Accumulated amortization = $33,000 = [($42,600 - $3,000) / 6] \times 5$

8-23 a)

	Patent	Copyright	License
Paid to purchase intangible	$60,000	$200,000	$320,000
Legal fees			24,000
Total cost	$60,000	$200,000	$344,000
Amortization period	5 years	8 years	40 years
Annual amortization	$12,000	$ 25,000	$ 8,600

b) Intangible assets

Patents [$60,000 - ($12,000 x 4)]	$ 12,000
Copyright [$200,000 - ($25,000 x 4]	100,000
License [$344,000 - ($8,600 x 4)]	309,600
Total intangible assets	$421,600

USER PERSPECTIVE SOLUTIONS

8-25 In making a long-term loan to a company, long-term assets such as plant and goodwill offer comfort to the lender so long as the company is operating as a going-concern, and does not appear to be experiencing financial difficulties. In this case, the long-term assets can generate cash flows in order to service and extinguish the long-term loan. However, if the ability of the company to continue into the indefinite future is in doubt, then the existence of long-term assets such as plant and goodwill offers less comfort to a lender. The liquidation value of such assets is likely to be much less than their value in use. In particular, the liquidation value of goodwill may be essentially zero.

8-27 After the acquisition, the UK company would present a smaller shareholders' equity on the balance sheet, reflecting the full deduction of the acquired goodwill. There would be no effect on the UK company's net income. On the other hand, the Canadian company could report lower net income in subsequent years because an impairment in value of goodwill hits the income statement. If the financial statement users fail to recognize this accounting difference, the UK company has an advantage because of higher net income in subsequent years and higher earnings per share reported each period. On the balance sheet the Canadian company would report an asset reflecting the value of goodwill judged not impaired. However, it is likely that financial analysts would not assign full economic value to this asset in evaluating a Canadian company's financial position.

8-29 As an accounting manager, you would attempt to allocate the purchase price between the land and the building on the basis of their relative fair values. You must allocate the purchase price between the assets because the land is not amortizable while the building is, so future income would be distorted if you failed to allocate the price in an appropriate manner. For tax purposes, your incentive would be to allocate as much as possible to the building so that you can deduct it as an expense over time. For reporting purposes, there is more incentive to capitalize the cost as a part of the land as this will result in higher net income being reported and reflect favorably upon your performance.

8-31 Depending on their age, none of the long-term assets will be properly valued on the books of the candidate company. The most suspect, however, would be the intangible assets such as goodwill. It is likely that you can make a fair assessment of the other assets by looking at market prices or doing an appraisal but the intangible assets will be much more difficult to evaluate. In addition, there are many intangible assets that will not be represented on the books of the company. Any internally generated intangible assets such as patents, trademarks, goodwill, human capital, etc. will have been expensed as incurred and will not be shown on the balance sheet.

8-33 **a)** Major changes in property, plant, and equipment are likely to result from the purchase or sale of an operating division or subsidiary. Because of the size of the reduction in property, plant, and equipment in 2003, it is likely that a major portion of its business has been discontinued or sold.

b) Fedders is primarily involved in the production and sale of room air conditioners for the home and business. The change in inventory levels could be due primarily to the change in weather conditions. During heat waves, sales depend on having air conditioning units available in the stores when the customer walks in. If the summer of 2002 was relatively cool, inventory levels could have built up in the distribution system. Then if the summer of 2003 was much hotter, more people would have purchased room air conditioners, thus drawing down the inventory levels. The company could have also installed a better inventory control system, permitting somewhat lower inventory levels to be held without losing sales

c) Goodwill represents the amount paid in excess of the fair value of the net assets acquired less the liabilities assumed when another company is purchased. It does not indicate that the company as a whole has excess earning power in an economic sense. Thus, the fact that losses were reported in 2002 and 2003 does not necessarily mean that the existing goodwill should be written off. More than two-thirds of the goodwill was eliminated from Fedder's balance sheet in 2003. If it discontinued a major portion of its business in 2003, as was suggested in part a), the goodwill associated with those operations would have been removed.

d) Gross profit and the gross profit ratio are important indicators of success. The asset turnover ratio and inventory turnover ratio also provide useful information in making comparisons over time and against other companies.

e) Although Fedders does not appear to be in a strong financial position at December 31, 2003, the reduced net loss indicates that operations during 2003 improved markedly over 2002. Before investing in Fedders, investors may seek information on a number of topics. The information given in the question does not indicate whether Fedders discontinued some operations. If it did, it would be interesting to know the impact it had on net income. It would also be helpful to look at the profit margins and sales volumes on the product line that was sold and those which were retained. Information on other operating attributes, debt maturities, cash flows, and comparative industry data also should be examined in evaluating the company. A complete annual report and any third-party reviews would be very beneficial in evaluating Fedders Company.

READING AND INTERPRETING PUBLISHED FINANCIAL STATEMENTS SOLUTIONS

8-35 a)   Research and development expense:
2001 – $31,428 x .20 = $6,286
2000 – $18,420 x .20 = $3,690
                          $9,976

MOSAID Technologies Incorporated
Consolidated Statement of Earnings and Retained Earnings
(in thousands, except per share amounts)

	Year Ended	
	Apr. 28, 2000	Apr. 27, 2001
Revenues		
Operations	$ 47,044	$ 81,640
Interest	1,065	1,286
	48,109	82,926
Expenses		
Labour and materials	8,181	13,367
Amortization of research & development	3,690	9,976
Selling and marketing	11,839	18,250
General and administration	7,015	8,338
Bad debt	—	139
Restructuring	(206)	694
	30,519	50,764
Earnings from operations	17,590	32,162
Income tax expense (Note 1)	(926)	(3,708)
Net earnings (loss)	16,664	28,454
Retained earnings, beginning of year	15,646	32,310
Retained earnings, end of year	$ 32,310	$ 60,764

Note 11: In re-constructing this income statement, the income taxes were not adjusted to reflect the higher income before income taxes because not enough information was given about

the tax rate. It is probable that the income tax would increase which would decrease net earnings.

b) Yes the results are significantly different. The net earnings in 2000 have increased from $1,904 to $16,664, an increase of $14,760. The net profit of $7,002 in 2001 has become a net profit of $28,454, an improvement of $21,452. Over the two years, net income would increase by $36,212—this represents costs moved to the balance sheet as the unamortized research and development costs:

2000 costs: $18,450 x 60% = $11,070
2001 costs: $31,428 x 80% =   <u>25,142</u>
                                       <u>$36,212</u>

c) Under GAAP, research costs must be expensed. Development costs can be capitalized if specific criteria are met. Because the future economic benefits of research and development are very difficult to determine, most research and development costs are expensed as they are incurred.

8-37 **a)** Purcell Energy uses the full cost method to account for oil and gas properties. This means that all of the costs associated with exploration and development of oil and gas properties are collected in an asset account and amortized (expensed) over time against the revenues from successful finds. These costs include "land acquisition costs, geological and geophysical expenses, carrying charges on non-producing properties, costs of drilling and overhead charges directly related to acquisition and exploration activities."

b) Yes, this method is what one would expect smaller oil and gas companies to use. The alternative, successful-efforts method would result in an uneven pattern of income from year to year, depending on how many successful wells are discovered each year.

c) Exploration costs each year = $80 million

1. Balance sheet value:

Year 1	Cost of 3 successful wells	$12 million
	Less: amort'n	(1.5) million
	[(12,000,000 x 300,000)/2,400,000]	
		$10.5 million

Year 2	Cost of Year 1 successful wells	$12 million
	Less: amort'n	(3) million
	[(12,000,000 x 600,000)/2,400,000]	
	Cost of Year 2 successful wells	12 million
	Less: amort'n	(1.5) million
	[(12,000,000 x 300,000)/2,400,000]	
		$19.5 million

2.

	Year 1	Year 2
Cost of unsuccessful wells (17 wells x $4 million)	$ 68 million	$ 68 million
Amortization of successful Wells	1.5 million	3 million
	$69.5 million	$71.0 million

8-39 a) The costs of major renewals and replacements are capitalized. These costs can include interest incurred during the renovation period. Maintenance, repairs, and minor renewals or replacements are expensed when incurred.

b) As noted in a), interest is capitalized during the construction period on new facilities and during the renovation period of major renovations to existing facilities costing over $1.0 million.

c) The costs of "circulating operating equipment" are capitalized and amortized by 33%. Replacements are expensed when placed in service.

d) Computer system development costs for internal use software are capitalized to the extent the project is expected to be of continuing benefit.

e) The costs associated with brand name and trademarks are amortized on a straight-line basis over 40 years. The recoverability of the unamortized costs of brand name and trademarks is evaluated on an annual basis to determine whether such costs will be recovered from future cash flows. If not, a writedown would be necessary.

CHAPTER 9

Liabilities

ASSESSING YOUR RECALL SOLUTIONS

9-1 The three essential characteristics of a liability are:
- The liability represents a duty or responsibility to transfer assets or services at a future date.
- The entity that is obligated has little or no discretion to avoid the future transfer.
- The transaction or event that gives rise to the obligation has already occurred.

9-3 Under GAAP, liabilities are valued at the net present value of the obligation. In the case of current liabilities, the difference between the gross amount and the net present value is so small that the gross amount is used. This makes the accounting entries easier and does not produce materially different amounts.

9-5 Unearned revenues are those revenues that have not yet the criteria for revenue recognition. Payments received magazine publisher for future copies of the magazine w an example. The unearned revenues are recognized a liabilities on the books of the seller until the revenue r criteria are met, at which time the liability is reduced revenue is recognized.

9-7 The current portion of long-term debt is that portion of long-term debt that is due within one year. It is recorded with the current liabilities because this portion of long-term debt must be paid off in the upcoming year. In order to present users of financial statements with a fair picture of all cash outflows that are expected to occur within one year of the balance sheet date, the current portion of long-term debt must be classified within current liabilities.

9-9 Loss contingencies may be recognized in the financial statements if two criteria are met. They are:
- Information available prior to the issuance of the financial statements indicates that it is likely that an asset has been impaired or that a liability has been incurred.
- The amount of the loss can be reasonably estimated.

Temporary differences: This term refers to differences in the carrying values of assets / liabilities as recorded in the accounting records versus those recorded in the tax records.

Permanent differences: This term refers to the difference that arises when a revenue or expense is recognized for book or tax purposes but not the other. This results in a permanent difference in the recognized revenues and expenses between the tax books and the accounting reporting books. Under GAAP, no future income taxes are recognized for these types of differences.

Differences: Originating and in the context of timing differences. timing, a difference between book but is reversed in a subsequent tization of an asset, the al cost allowance) is xpense for book set's life. This would

8. SE-Interest expense   1,500
        A-Cash ($20,000 x 7.5%)   1,500
    L-Bank loan (long-term)   4,000
        L-Current portion of LT debt   4,000

b) Current Liabilities:
    Accounts payable $118,700
    Wages payable   5,700
    Interest payable   87
    Unearned revenue   1,500
    Obligations under warranties   26,900
    Short-term loan   35,000
    Current portion of long-term debt   4,000
                                               $191,887

c) $4,000 of the 5-year bank loan represents the current portion of long-term debt because it requires the use of current assets and must be paid during the upcoming year. The remaining $16,000 does not require the use of current assets, and is thus classified as part of long-term liabilities.

9-15 a) and b) Journal entries

   Aug.   A-Cash   20,000
                 L-Unearned advertising revenue   20,000

   Sept.   A-Cash (3,000 x $16)   48,000
                 L-Unearned subscription revenue   48,000

   To Dec.   A-Cash (5,000 x $2.75 x 4 months)   55,000
                 SE-Magazine revenue   55,000

             SE-Printing expense   66,000
                 A-Cash   66,000

Adjusting journal entries

L-Unearned advertising revenue	10,000	
SE-Advertising revenue ($20,000 x 4/8 issues)		10,000
L-Unearned subscription revenue	24,000	
SE-Subscription revenue ($48,000 x 4/8 issues)		24,000

Alternatively, the original entries for advertising and subscriptions could have been:

- Recorded as revenues, and an adjustment made to reduce the revenues and recognize one half of these amounts as unearned revenues at December 31.
- Recorded as one half earned and one half unearned. Then no adjusting entries would be required on December 31.

c)

University Survival Magazine
Income Statement
For the four months ended December 31, 2003

Revenue:	
Subscription revenue	$ 24,000
Magazine revenue	55,000
Advertising revenue	10,000
Total revenue	$89,000
Printing expense	66,000
Net income	$ 23,000

APPLYING YOUR KNOWLEDGE SOLUTIONS

9-13 a)

1.	A-Computer system	31,500	
	L-Accounts payable		28,000
	A-Cash		3,500
2.	A-Inventory	94,000	
	L-Accounts payable		94,000
	L-Accounts payable	86,000	
	A-Cash		86,000
3.	A-Cash	35,000	
	L-Short-term loan		35,000
	SE-Interest expense	87	
	L-Interest payable		87
	($35,000 x .06 x 0.5/12)		
4.	L-Rent payable	24,000	
	SE-Rent expense	12,000	
	A-Cash		36,000
5.	L-Unearned revenue	3,000	
	SE-Revenue		3,000
6.	SE-Warranty expense	15,000	
	L-Obligations under warranties		15,000
	L-Obligations under warranties	1,100	
	A-Cash		1,100
7.	SE-Wages expense	5,700	
	L-Wages payable		5,700

result in an originating difference. In the last half of the asset's life the amortization expense for book purposes will be higher than for tax purposes, resulting in a reversing difference.

d) Cash balance = $20,000 + $48,000 + $55,000 - $66,000 = $57,000

To: University Survival Magazine Owners
From: Your name, Accountant
Re: Results of operations to December 31, 2003

The results of operation to December 31, 2003 is a net income of $23,000. This is substantially less than the current bank balance of $57,000. The reason for this difference is that revenues are recorded only when they are earned. The cash from both the subscriptions and the advertising was put in the bank when it was received, but the revenue recognized from these two items needs to be spread out over the eight months for which the company has an obligation to print the magazine. Therefore, the revenue from the subscriptions and advertising represents only half of the cash that was received. The cash in the bank of $57,000 is $34,000 higher than the net income of $23,000 as there are unearned revenues of $10,000 and $24,000 on the balance sheet, representing, respectively, cash received from advertisers and subscribers.

9-17 a) Warranty expense matched to 2004 revenue:

Defective in 2004 (10,000 x 1% x $50)	$ 5,000
Defective in 2005 (10,000 x 2% x $50)	10,000
Defective in 2006 (10,000 x 3% x $50)	15,000
	$30,000
Less: 2004 actual payments	(6,000)
Estimated warranty obligation Dec. 31, 2004	$24,000

b) Warranty expense matched to 2005 revenue:

Defective in 2005 (15,000 x 1% x $50)	$ 7,500
Defective in 2006 (15,000 x 2% x $50)	15,000
Defective in 2007 (15,000 x 3% x $50)	22,500
Warranty expense – 2005	$45,000

c)

Expected	Actual Cash Cash Payments	Difference Payments	Over (under)
2004	$ 5,000	$ 6,000	$ 1,000
2005:			
on 2004 sales	10,000		
on 2005 sales	7,500		
	$17,500	20,000	2,500
2006:			
on 2004 sales	15,000		
on 2005 sales	15,000		
on 2006 sales	20,000		
	$50,000	49,000	(1,000)

The company's estimates with respect to warranty costs seem to be higher than expected in 2004 and 2005 but lower in 2006, with the cumulative costs higher than expected. The company may wish to increase its estimates of defect rates in the three-year warranty period. However, the company is being conservative and may wish to wait a few more years to be sure the pattern continues before making an adjustment.

9-19 a) Liability method
Straight-line:
Annual book amortization = ($38,000 - $2,000) / 8
= $4,500 per year

Year 20x1:

	Book	Tax
Income before amortization and tax	$80,000	$80,000
Amortization / CCA	4,500	3,800[1]
Income before taxes	75,500	76,200
Taxes @ 30%		22,860

Tax expense:
Current	22,860
Future	(210)[2]
Tax expense	22,650
Net Income	$52,850

[1] $3,800 = $38,000 x 20% x ½
[2] $210 = [($38,000 - $4,500) − ($38,000 - $3,800)] x 30%

SE-Current tax expense	22,860	
L-Tax payable		22,860
A-Future income tax asset	210	
SE-Future tax expense		210

Year 20x2:

	Book	Tax
Income before amortization and tax	$80,000	$80,000
Amortization / CCA	4,500	
		6,840[1]
Income before taxes	75,500	73,160
Taxes @ 30%		21,948
Tax expense:		
Current	21,948	
Future	702[2]	
Tax expense	22,650	
Net Income	$52,850	

[1] $6,840 = (38,000 - 3,800) x 20%
[2] ($702) = ($210) − [($33,500 - $4,500) − ($34,200 - $6,840)] x 30%

SE-Current tax expense	21,948	
L-Current tax payable		21,948
SE-Future tax expense	702	
A-Future tax asset		210
L-Future tax liability		492

b) For 20x1, $210 appears under the account title *Future income tax asset*, and for 20x2, $492 appears under the account title *Future income tax liability*. The *Future income tax asset* account is classified as other assets on the balance sheet, and the *Future income tax liability* account is classified as other liabilities on the balance sheet.

c) Because there is a net *Future income tax liability* account, it means that the company has used up more of the tax benefit from purchasing the asset than is reflected in the book value of the asset. In other words, the book value of the asset is greater than the undepreciated capital cost (UCC), so less of a tax deduction is left for future years. As a banker, you should regard this as an expected future cash outflow that occurs as the result of deducting less CCA in the future, and thus paying more tax.

9-21 a)

	Tax
Income before amortization and tax	$ 400,000
CCA ($500,000 x 20% x ½)	50,000
Income before taxes	$ 350,000
Taxes @ 45%	$ 157,500

b) CCA [from a)] = $50,000; Amortization = $60,000
As the tax book value (UCC) of $450,000 is greater than the accounting book value of $440,000, this creates a future income tax asset. The future tax rate of 40% is used, as this will be the value of the temporary difference when it reverses.

Future income tax asset = [($500,000 – 50,000) – ($500,000 – 60,000)] x 40%
= $4,000

c) This future income tax represents the value of future income tax savings. A smaller deduction for the usage of the asset was claimed on the 2003 tax return than for accounting purposes. This means that a larger deduction will be possible on the tax return in the future, resulting in a decrease in future taxes payable.

d) 2003 income tax expense:

Taxes payable @ 45%	$ 157,500
Increase to future tax asset	(4,000)
	$ 153,500

e) 2004 CCA = ($500,000 – 50,000) x 20%
= $90,000

f)

2004 CCA	$ 90,000
2004 amortization	70,000
	$ 20,000
	x 40%
	$ 8,000

g) Decrease in future tax asset (of $4,000) to zero, and creation of $4,000 future tax liability:

SE–Future tax expense	8,000	
A-Future tax asset		4,000
L-Future tax liability		4,000

h) The balance in the future income tax account represents the difference between the assets' UCC (carrying value of asset for tax purposes) and net book value (for accounting purposes) multiplied by the tax rate expected to be in effect when the timing differences reverse. If UCC < NBV this results in a future income tax liability.

At end of 2004:
UCC ($500,000 – 50,000 – 90,000) $360,000
NBV ($500,000 – 60,000 – 70,000)   370,000
                                          $ 10,000
                                            x 40%
Future tax liability $ 4,000

USER PERSPECTIVE SOLUTIONS

9-23 As a stock analyst, you should look at a future tax liability as a real future obligation of the company to pay taxes in excess of the tax rate applied to accounting income. In other words, because of temporary differences that originated in the past, taxable income is going to exceed accounting income in the future and the company is going to pay more income tax to the Canada Customs and Revenue Agency. However, a future tax liability is different than a long-term bank loan because there is more uncertainty regarding both the amount and the timing of the obligation. For example, if a company continues to invest in fixed assets, then the undepreciated capital cost is going to be less than the accounting book value year after year, so that the future tax liability continues to increase.

9-25 **a)** The sweeteners create a legal obligation of the company even though they may not be recorded at the time of signing of the agreement since they could be viewed as mutually unexecuted contracts. They have the potential, however, to result in losses to the company if economic conditions change and the company finds itself in a situation where it must deliver raw materials at a fixed price.

b) As long as the current market price of the raw materials is at or below the contract price that is fixed there is little to record relative to these contracts as they would be viewed as mutually unexecuted.

c) Our answer to b) would change if the market price exceeded the contract price. With each delivery the company would suffer a loss and the company should accrue a loss on all of the contracts when it can reasonably estimate the amount.

d) Shareholders should probably have some awareness of the existence of these contracts since they have the potential to create losses for the company. As mutually unexecuted contracts they are typically not recorded, but footnote disclosures could clearly be given.

READING AND INTERPRETING PUBLISHED FINANCIAL STATEMENTS SOLUTIONS

9-27 a) For producing properties, the estimated costs for reclamation are estimated and expensed over the life of the estimated reserves. The costs of reclamation are part of the cost associated with generating the revenue from the producing properties and therefore it is appropriate that these costs be matched against the revenue as it is generated. For non-producing properties, the costs are accrued as liabilities when the costs are likely to be incurred and can be reasonably estimated. Actual site reclamation costs are deducted from the liability. The non-producing properties are not generating revenue. so it is not possible to match these costs to anything. It is therefore appropriate that they be expensed as soon as they are known.

b) Part of the cost associated with the revenue generated from producing properties is the cost of cleaning up and restoring the property after the revenue generation is complete. It is therefore appropriate to match these costs against the revenue as it occurs. It is not appropriate to wait until the actual costs are incurred because at that time there is no revenue against which to generate these costs.

9-29 a) Customer deposits represent the amounts that clients have given to Investors Group to be invested. Investors Group has an obligation to return funds if their clients withdraw their investments.

b) Liabilities such as customer deposits are likely long-term because most clients would be interested in leaving their funds with Investors Group to manage over an extended period of time. Customers could, however, withdraw their funds within a short period of time, which gives the assets a short-term aspect. As the timing of customer withdrawals is uncertain, Investors Group does not distinguish between current and non-current liabilities. However the balance sheet description of liabilities such as long-term debt assists users in assessing liquidity.

c) This asset implies that Investors Group is involved in loaning out money. It is listed with the assets because it represents the future mortgage payments that will be made to the company in repayment of mortgage money borrowed. To Investors Group, this is an asset.

9-31 **a)** Dofasco's statutory rate for income tax in:
2001   42.98%   ($24.2/$56.3)
2000   43.90%   ($114.4/$260.6)

b) The actual tax rates:
2001   52.04%   ($29.3/$56.3)
2000   30.00%   ($78.2/$$260.6)

c) In 2001 Dofasco actually paid $61.5 million in income tax to the Canada Customs and Revenue Agency, and $107.4 million in 2000. These amounts are shown as the current amount in the first table of the exhibit.

d) Permanent differences are differences between accounting and tax reporting that never reverse themselves. An accounting item that will never become a tax item, or a tax item that will never become an accounting item. The manufacturing and processing credit is a deduction allowed for tax purposes but it is not an expense in the accounting records. The benefit of previously unrecognized losses of U.S. subsidiaries is also a deduction allowed for tax purposes, but is not an expense for accounting purposes.

9-33 **a)** The "guaranteeing of indebtedness of third parties" means that the company has agreed to act as a guarantor for other companies. If those companies default on outstanding commitments, the creditor can come to Alcan to collect the amount owed.

b) It was important for Alcan to include a note about the guarantees because there is a possibility that Alcan could be required to pay these amounts in the future if the third parties default. Financial statement users need to know about this possibility.

c) These commitments for the supplies of goods and services represent mutually unexecuted contracts. As either side acts on the conditions of these contracts—delivers goods, performs services, pays in advance or amounts owed—the actions are recorded in the accounting system. Prior to such actions, nothing is recorded unless there is a likelihood of future losses associated with these contracts. The fact that they are described in the commitment sections of the notes indicates that they have not been recorded in the accounting system.

d) Answers will depend on any recent developments.

BEYOND THE BOOK SOLUTIONS

9-35 Answers to this question will depend on the company selected.

CHAPTER 10

Long-Term Liabilities

ASSESSING YOUR RECALL SOLUTIONS

10-1 Indenture Agreement: A formal agreement between a borrowing entity and lender that specifies the terms of the contract. In the case of a bond offering, it specifies (among other things) the face value, the maturity date, the interest rate, the collateral, and the covenants.

Bond Covenants: Provisions included in an indenture agreement that restrict the borrowing entity in some way. Typically these covenants would restrict the ability of the borrowing entity to pay dividends or to obtain additional borrowings. The restrictions often take the form of restrictions on the level of certain ratios. For instance, a covenant may state that the company must maintain a current ratio of at least 2.

Face Value: The measure of denomination of a bond. Typically a single bond has a face value of $1,000. For bonds, the face value also determines the cash payout at maturity and is used to determine the periodic interest payments.

Maturity Date: The date at which the bond pays back the face value and the date at which interest payments cease.

Bond Interest Rate: A percentage that is used to determine the periodic interest payments that a bond provides. The rate is multiplied by the face value to determine the total annual payout.

Interest Payments: The periodic payments that a bond provides. The payments are typically paid at the end of each six-month period through the maturity date. The amount of the payment is calculated by multiplying the face value by the bond interest rate and dividing by two (assuming semiannual payments).

Collateral: Assets that the borrower pledges to the lender in the event that the borrower defaults on the loan.

10-3   The stated or nominal rate of interest on a bond is also known as the bond interest rate. It determines the amount of the semi-annual interest payments (face value x bond interest rate / 2). This is not the same as the effective or real rate of interest (also known as the yield rate) unless the bond is sold at par. The yield rate is the interest rate demanded by the buyer for his investment.

10-5   The term "best efforts basis" means that the investment bankers will make their best effort to attempt to sell the bonds that the borrower is offering to their clients. In the event that the bonds become unattractive to their clients or there is very little demand for these bonds, the bonds are returned to the borrower. The impact on the company is that there is no guarantee that it will be able to raise the amount of financing it wants.

10-7   The terms par, premium, and discount refer to whether the selling price of a bond is at, above, or below the face value of the bond. For a typical bond with a $1,000 face value it would sell at par if its selling price is $1,000, at a premium if the selling price is above $1,000, and at a discount if the selling price is below $1000.

10-9   When debt is retired before maturity, the cost to settle the debt is compared with the current carrying value of the debt on the books. The difference between these two amounts represents a gain or loss on the retirement of the debt. A company may choose to retire debt early because interest rates have dropped and it can borrow today at a lower interest rate. It will borrow at a lower rate and use the proceeds to pay off the higher interest cost debt. Another reason for retiring debt early may be to use available cash to settle the debt so that future interest payments do not have to be made.

10-11 GAAP specifies the criteria for a capital lease. If *any one* of the following is met, the lease qualifies as a capital lease.

1. The title to the asset passes to the lessee by the end of the lease term
2. The lease term is equal to or greater than 75% of the useful life of the asset.
3. The present value of the minimum lease payments is greater than 90% of the fair value of the leased asset.

The first criteria would indicate that the title to the asset will pass to the buyer by the end of the lease term and, therefore, the asset is being purchased by the lessee. The last two criteria indicate that the company will have use of the asset during most of its useful life even though title does not necessarily pass to the lessee. The substance of the transaction is, therefore, a purchase.

10-13 Overfunded – An overfunded pension plan is one in which the value of the assets held in trust exceeds the value of the liabilities to pay benefits.

Underfunded – An underfunded pension plan is one in which the value of the assets held in trust is less than the value of the liabilities to pay benefits.

Fully funded – A fully funded pension plan is one in which the value of the assets held in trust equals the value of the liabilities to pay benefits.

10-15 The debt/equity ratio measures the amount of assets that are financed through debt. If a company is carrying too much debt it will run the risk of being unable to meets its interest and debt payments. The times interest earned ratio measures the company's ability to meet its interest payment from operating income.

APPLYING YOUR KNOWLEDGE SOLUTIONS

10-17 a) Journal entry for issuance:

A-Cash	937,689	
XL-Discount on bonds payable	62,311	
L-Bonds payable		1,000,000

b) Journal entries for interest expense in Year 1:
    Interest payments: $1,000,000 \times 9\% \times 6/12 = \$45,000$
    Interest expense on June 30, 2001: $937,689 \times 10\% \times 6/12$
                           $= \$46,884$
    Interest expense on Dec. 31, 2001: ($937,689 + \$46,884 -$
                           $\$45,000) \times 10\% \times 6/12$
                           $= \$46,979$

        Total interest expense for Year 1 = \$46,884 + \$46,979
                                  = \$93,863

June 30	SE-Interest expense	46,884	
	A-Cash		45,000
	XL-Discount on bonds payable		1,884

Dec. 31	SE-Interest expense	46,979	
	A-Cash		45,000
	XL-Discount on bonds payable		1,979

c) Investors were not willing to pay $1,000,000 for the bonds because the interest rate required for the risk that investors bear (the yield of 10%) exceeds the interest rate offered on the bonds (9%). Consequently, the bonds sell at less than their par value, and the company is not able to raise the $1,000,000 that it had hoped for.

10-19 a) 1st issue: $\$400,000 \times 10\%$ = $\qquad$ $\$40,000$
$\qquad$ 2nd issue: $\$300,000 \times 6\%$ = $\qquad$ $\underline{18,000}$
$\qquad$ Total 2004 payments $\qquad$ $\underline{\$58,000}$

b) Issue price for 1st issue $\quad$ = PV of interest payments + PV of
$\qquad$ maturity repayment
$\qquad$ = $PV_AF_{4\%,14} \times \$20,000 + PVF_{4\%,14} \times$
$\qquad$ $\$400,000$
$\qquad$ = $\$442,254$

$\qquad$ Issue price for 2nd issue $\quad$ = PV of interest payments + PV of
$\qquad$ maturity repayment
$\qquad$ = $PV_AF_{4\%,10} \times \$9,000 + PVF_{4\%,10} \times$
$\qquad$ $\$300,000$
$\qquad$ = $\$275,666$

$\qquad$ 1st issue, interest expense for 2003: $\$17,690 + \$17,598$
$\qquad$ = $\$35,288$

$\qquad$ 1st issue, interest expense for 2004: $\$17,502 + \$17,402$
$\qquad$ = $\$34,904$

$\qquad$ 2nd issue, interest expense for 2004: $\$11,027 + \$11,108$
$\qquad$ = $\$22,135$

$\qquad$ Total interest expense for 2004 = $\$34,904$ (1st issue) +
$\qquad$ $\$22,135$ (2nd issue)
$\qquad$ = $\$57,039$

b) Journal entries for 2004
July 1, 2004 $\quad$ SE-Interest expense $\qquad$ 17,502
$\qquad$ L-Premium on bonds payable $\quad$ 2,498
$\qquad$ A-Cash $\qquad$ 20,000

$\qquad$ SE-Interest expense $\qquad$ 11,027
$\qquad$ XL-Discount on bonds payable $\qquad$ 2,027
$\qquad$ A-Cash $\qquad$ 9,000

Dec. 31, 2004 SE-Interest expense   17,402
                 L-Premium on bonds payable   2,598
                 L-Interest payable   20,000

            SE-Interest expense   11,108
                 XL-Discount on bonds payable   2,108
                 L-Interest payable   9,000

d) It is reasonable that both bond issues are sold to yield 8% because different bond issues of the same company bear the same default risk, so long as nothing significant has occurred since the first issue that would cause investors to demand a different yield rate.

10-21 a) Issue price $= PV_AF_{4\%,16} \times (\$500,000 \times 10\% \times 6/12) + PVF_{4\%,16}$
                                $\times \$500,000$
                                $= 11.65230 \times \$25,000 + 0.53391 \times \$500,000$
                                $= \$291,308 + \$266,955$
                                $= \$558,263$

A-Cash   558,263
    L-Premium on bonds payable   58,263
    L-Bonds payable   500,000

Interest expense for 1st year
  = \$558,263 x 8% x 6/12 + (\$558,263 + \$22,331 −\$25,000)
     x 8% x 6/12
  = \$22,331 + 22,224
  = \$44,555

Book value, end of 1st year = \$558,263 + \$44,555 − \$50,000
                                = \$552,818

b) Interest expense for 2nd year
  = \$552,818 x 8% x 6/12 + (\$552,818 + \$22,113 - \$25,000)
    x 8% x 6/12
  = \$22,113 + \$21,997
  = \$44,110

Book value, end of 2nd year = \$552,818 + \$44,110 - \$50,000
                                 = \$546,928

c) Market value of bonds = PV of Interest Payments + PV of
    Maturity Payment
      = $PV_AF_{6\%,12}$ x \$25,000 + $PVF_{6\%,12}$ x \$500,000
      = 8.38384 x \$25,000 + 0.49697 x \$500,000
      = \$458,081

(NOTE: n= 12 semi-annual periods remaining, yield = 6%
per period)

d) The difference between the book value and market value of
    the bonds is \$88,847 (\$546,928 – \$458,081). The difference
    is attributable to the fact that the interest rate that investors
    require has increased from 8% to 12%. Consequently the
    price of the bonds fell.

e) L-Bonds Payable   500,000
    L-Premium on Bonds Payable   46,928
      A-Cash   458,081
      SE-Gain on Redemption of Bonds   88,847
          Payable

10-23 Journal entries:

July 1, 2003 A-Machine under capital lease[1]   750,000
                  L-Capital lease obligation   750,000

Dec. 31, 2003   SE-Interest expense[2]   52,500
                  L-Capital lease obligation   18,295
                  A-Cash   70,795

                  SE-Amortization expense[3]   37,500
                  XA-Accumulated amortization   37,500

June 30, 2004   SE-Interest expense[4]   51,219
                  L-Capital lease obligation   19,576
                  A-Cash   70,795

Dec. 31, 2004   SE-Interest expense[5]   49,849
                  L-Capital lease obligation   20,946
                  A-Cash   70,795

                  SE-Amortization expense   75,000
                  XA-Accumulated amortization   75,000

[1]$750,000 = present value of 20 semiannual payments of $70,795 discounted at 7% per period = 10.59401 x $70,795
[2] $52,500 = $750,000 x 14% x 1/2
[3]$37,500 = (750,000 / 10) x ½
[4]($750,000 – $18,295) x 14% x ½ = $51,219
[5]($750,000 - $18,295 - $19,576)x 14% x ½ = $49,849

10-25 a) *Provincial Star* should account for this lease as an operating lease because none of the criteria for capitalization appear to be satisfied. Title to the asset does not revert to the lessee at the end of the lease, the lease term only spans 30% of the truck's economic life, and the present value of the minimum lease payments is less than 90% of the fair market value of the truck.

b) *Provincial Star* should account for this lease as a capital lease. Title to the asset does not revert to the lessee at the end of the lease, the lease term only spans 60% of the truck's economic life, but the present value of the minimum lease payments is 92.9% of the fair market value of the truck ($22,000). Thus the third capital lease criteria is met.

PV of minimum lease payments
$= PV_AF_{0.75\%,36}$ x $650
= 31.44681 x $650
= $20,440

c) Operating lease method

Jan. 31, 2004	SE-Lease expense	650	
	A-Cash		650
Feb. 28, 2004	SE-Lease expense	650	
	A-Cash		650

Capital lease method

Jan. 31, 2004	SE-Interest expense[1]	153	
	L-Capital lease obligation	497	
	A-Cash		650
	SE-Amortization expense[2]	568	
	XA-Accumulated amortization		568
Feb. 28, 2004	SE-Interest expense[3]	150	
	L-Capital lease obligation	500	
	A-Cash		650
	SE-Amortization expense	568	
	XA-Accumulated amortization		568

[1]PV of $650 for 36 periods at 9/12% = $650 x 31.44681
= $20,440 $20,440 x .09 x 1/12 = $153
[2]$20,440 / 36 = $568
[3]$150 = ($20,440 + $153 - $650) x .09 x 1/12

USER PERSPECTIVE SOLUTIONS

10-27 To protect their investment, bond investors like covenants in the indenture agreement. These include such restrictions on the company as maintaining a minimum current ratio or maximum debt to equity ratio, or restricting the declaration of dividends. Such covenants prevent the company from imposing additional risk on bondholders through the issuance of additional debt, or diluting the assets of the company through payments to shareholders.

10-29 As a lender, plant and equipment give me some level of comfort as collateral for a long-term loan although the value depends on how specialized and how marketable the plant and equipment might be. Goodwill and other intangibles give a lot less comfort as they are not readily marketable assets. Their value depends on finding a willing buyer to pay more than the estimated fair value of the other assets of the company.

10-31 The decision to treat a lease as operating or capital does not significantly affect net income, because the rent expense recorded in an operating lease is often similar to the total of amortization expense and interest expense recorded for capital leases. However, if you are in the early years of a lease, there is an incentive to treat the lease as operating, because capital leases result in higher interest expense and amortization expense (assuming use of the declining balance method) when the obligation and asset are new.

10-33 Pension plans can be defined contribution plans or defined benefit plans. In a defined contribution plan, the employer contributes a set amount each period to the pension plan, and the amount that retirees are entitled to is contingent upon the performance and management of the plan assets. In a defined benefit plan, the employer defines the actual amount that retirees are entitled to in their retirement years, so if the plan assets are insufficient, the employer is responsible. From the perspective of a company, a defined contribution plan is preferred, because the exact obligation of the company is defined, and employees bear the consequences if the pension assets fail to appreciate. From the perspective of an employee, the defined benefit plan is preferred, because you can be certain as to the amount you are entitled to, regardless of economic conditions, interest rates, and the performance of plan assets.

10-35 Liabilities that might not appear on the financial statements include uncertain contingent losses, potential product liability losses, and off-balance-sheet financing such as operating leases or factoring of accounts receivable when the factor has recourse if amounts cannot be collected. Information included in the notes should list contingent losses to the extent that these losses are probable but not estimable. Future commitments relating to operating leases and factoring should also be disclosed in the notes.

READING AND INTERPRETING PUBLISHED FINANCIAL STATEMENTS

10-37 All amounts in millions

    a) A senior subordinated note is a note that has senior claim on resources ahead of some other debt instruments such as the subordinated debentures, but ranks behind all of the company's existing and future senior indebtedness. Subordinated debentures have claim on resources only after satisfaction of all senior indebtedness, including the senior subordinated notes.

    b) Apr. 30   SE-Interest expense[1]   4.97

                    L-Interest payable   4.97

[1]$€4.97 = €145 \times 11.75\% \times 3.5 / 12$

          July 15   SE-Interest expense[2]   3.55

                     L-Interest payable   4.97

                     A-Cash   8.52

[2]$€3.55 = €145 \times 11.75\% \times 2.5 / 12$

    c) The company would want to exercise its redemption option if interest rates fall, so that cheaper debt financing can be obtained. If interest rates fall, the company could obtain another loan at a lower interest rate, and use the proceeds to redeem the existing higher interest rate debt. Or, if the company determines that it has excess cash, it might redeem the debt in order to cease the interest payments for funds it no longer needs.

    d) The debentures appear to be unsecured because both are subordinated. This means that there are no specific assets pledged as security against the debt.

10-39 a) The interest rate on the capital leases is higher than the interest rate on the medium-term notes or the bankers' acceptances because the capital leases were probably not arranged through a financial institution. A lessor often attempts to earn a return on its assets similar to what other assets in the lessor's company earn. This probably means a higher rate of interest than is charged by a financial institution to a good customer. Also, lessors may be in the business of manufacturing capital equipment, not lending money, so will charge a higher interest rate as they may not have many lease arrangements and so cannot spread the risk of default among as many customers as a bank.

b) Users need to know the principal repayments for debt over the next five years so that they can evaluate the future cash flow needs of the company.

10-41 a) Aliant has both kinds of pensions, defined benefit and defined contribution. The company also offers life insurance and healthcare plans as non-pension post-employment benefits.

b) At the end of 2001, the value of the fund assets is less than the value of the obligation by $60,002,000, so the plan is underfunded.

c) The balance sheet showed an accrued benefit asset of $95,127,000 related to its pension benefit plans, and a liability of $138,885,000 related to other benefit plans.

d) The company's pension expense calculations require estimation of discount rate, expected rate of return on plan assets and employee salary changes. It appears as if the company's past estimates may not have been accurate and were changed, leading to an actuarial loss, which is being amortized to the accrued benefit obligation. Thus the cash contributions to the plan's assets may not match the amount of the accrued benefit obligation.

10-43 a) (in millions)

	2001	2000
Total liabilities	$23,639	$25,223
Total assets	$27,689	$28,253
Debt / Equity ratio	**85.4%**	**89.3%**

b) The report should include the following point:
- Between 2000 and 2001, Xerox decreased its debt / equity ratio, which means that less of its total assets are financed through the use of debt. The main reasons for the decrease in this ratio are the $1,872 decrease in short-term and long-term debt, while assets declined by only $564. The reduction in debt and debt/equity ratio would signal a slightly safer investment. High levels of debt reduce a company's flexibility when cash is tight, as interest and debt repayment schedules are usually fixed. This may be of concern to Xerox investors as the reduction in retained earnings indicates the company experienced a loss in 2001.

BEYOND THE BOOK SOLUTION

10-45 Answers to this question will depend on the company selected.

CHAPTER 11

Shareholders' Equity

ASSESSING YOUR RECALL SOLUTIONS

11-1   The forms of business organization that have limited legal liability as a benefit are:
    Corporations
    Limited Partnership

The forms of business organization that are exempt from corporate taxation (i.e. the income is only taxed once at the personal level) are:
    Sole-proprietorships
    Partnerships
    Limited partnerships

11-3 The articles of incorporation specify the type of business, the operating structure and the officers of the business, and the structure of the share capital of the business. They specify the authorized classes and numbers of shares. The only major significant item for the accounting system is the specification of the different classes of shares.

11-5 Preferred shares differ from common shares in that they are given a preference with regard to dividends. Preferred shares must be paid dividends first before common shares are entitled to receive dividends. Preferred shares also have different rights from the basic rights of the common shares. Typically, the preferred shares are non-voting or carry a lesser right to vote (for instance, a half a vote per share). If the corporation decides to liquidate, preferred shareholders usually have a claim on assets prior to the claim of common shareholders. There are many other features of preferred shares that are different from common shares. See Problem 6 for a list.

11-7 Authorized shares are the maximum number of shares the corporation is permitted to issue. Issued shares are the shares the corporation has actually sold to shareholders. Outstanding shares are the shares owned by shareholders, excluding treasury shares owned by the corporation.

11-9 Property dividends are satisfied through the transfer of property rather than through the transfer of cash. These are not used often because the property transferred might not be separable into equal units, making it difficult for each shareholder to get a proportionate amount based on the number of shares he or she holds.

11-11 A 100% stock dividend and a 2 for 1 split have the same economic effect on the corporation. Twice as many shares will be outstanding after the transaction as before. There is no change in total shareholders' equity under either.

11-13 Companies issue stock options to employees as an incentive to work to increase the market value of the corporation. If employees are also shareholders, they may work harder to make the corporation a success. The exercise price of the option is typically set at a value slightly above the current market value of the shares to provide the necessary incentive. Typically these types of options have no effects on the financial statements at the date they are issued because they are not instantly valuable (because the exercise price is higher than the current share price). The only effect they have is when they are exercised and the corporation has to issue shares to satisfy the options. This causes more shares to be outstanding and could dilute the earnings per share number. For this reason, the fully diluted earnings per share calculation incorporates the shares that can potentially have a future dilutive effect due to share options.

11-15 The price/earnings ratio indicates to users the market price of a share compared to the book earnings per share. The ratio thus reflects the importance, as reflected in the market price, of one dollar of earnings in a company.

APPLYING YOUR KNOWLEDGE SOLUTIONS

11-17 a) A dental practice of five dentists is likely to be a partnership. The earnings of the organization will depend on the individual client base of each of the dentists. They would therefore probably prefer to receive earnings in relation to their efforts. A partnership works best for this.

b) A chain of clothing stores in which all of the stores are owned by the same company would probably be a corporation. Expansion from one location to another usually requires more capital than one individual can raise. Issuing shares to other investors (forming a corporation) is an efficient way of raising additional capital. Individual shops might be owned locally as sole proprietorships operating under license from the company that owns the idea for the chain (the license is called a franchise).

c) A paint and body shop owned by one person is likely to be a sole proprietorship. The owner would probably manage the shop and a sole proprietorship is easy to establish.

d) A lumber company operating in British Columbia is likely to be a corporation. The resources required to establish a lumber company would likely be more than one person could raise. Issuing shares to other investors (forming a corporation) is an efficient way of raising the necessary capital.

e) A family-owned farm is likely to be a partnership among the three brothers. A partnership would allow each of the brothers to have an equal say in the operations of the farm.

f) A lobster fisher is likely to be a sole proprietorship. The fisher would manage the operation and would want an organizational structure that is easy to set up and manage

11-19 a) Operating as a sole proprietorship does not require coordination with other owners and there is no confusion as to who profits if the business is financially successful and who loses if it is not. Albert would not need to negotiate with others about who will undertake which duties and which responsibilities will be assumed by whom. He also may be able to focus more easily on the types of services he would like to provide. He will however, be limited to his own personal resources when it comes to raising new capital.

b) The corporate form of organization provides certain protection for personal assets because of its limited liability feature. Also, it is normally easier to raise larger amounts of capital to purchase equipment or facilities in which to operate using the corporate form. However, as a new and unproven businessperson, he may have difficulty raising large amounts of capital. There may also be tax advantages in that he will be taxed at the corporate rate which could be lower then his personal income tax rate. Once he is established as a corporation he could raise capital by issuing shares to others, which would expand his potential new capital base.

c) Many customers are likely to be indifferent about the form of business. If given a preference, they might prefer an incorporated business, because a corporation has a separate existence from the owner and can thus continue to operate into the indefinite future. This might be important for a software company, because customers are more comfortable that an incorporated company is going to be around in the future to satisfy warranties and support its products.

d) Creditors might also prefer a corporation because a corporation has a separate existence from the owner and can thus continue to operate into the indefinite future. The separate existence will make it easier to identify corporate assets that may be used to settle creditor payments. It may also be easier for a corporation to raise capital, which would reassure creditors about receiving payment.

e) If Albert anticipates rapid growth in his business, the corporate form of organization is most appropriate because it is easier for him to raise capital through the issuance of shares. Capital is likely to be required to finance the expansion that he anticipates.

11-21 a) 1. Information on the number of common and preferred shares authorized will be reported in the shareholders' equity section of the balance sheet. No journal entry is made until actual shares are issued.

    2. The following journal entry will be recorded when the common shares are issued:

A-Cash (90,000 x $12)	1,080,000	
SE-Common shares (90,000 x $12)		1,080,000

    3. The following journal entry will be recorded when the preferred shares are issued:

A-Cash (25,000 x $18)	450,000	
SE-Preferred shares (25,000 x $18)		450,000

    4. The following journal entry will be recorded when the preferred dividend is declared and paid:

SE-Preferred dividends declared		
(25,000 x $2.50)	62,500	
A-Cash (25,000 x $2.50)		62,500

5. The following entry will be recorded when the common dividend is declared:

SE-Dividends declared		
(90,000 x $0.25)	22,500	
L-Dividends payable (90,000 x $0.25)		22,500

6. Retained earnings will increase by $220,000 and total shareholders' equity will increase by $220,000.

SE-Income summary	220,000	
SE-Retained earnings		220,000

7. The following journal entry is recorded when the dividend is paid on the common shares:

L-Dividends payable	22,500	
A-Cash		22,500

8. A 5% stock dividend is declared and distributed on the common shares:

SE-Dividends declared		
(90,000 x 5% x $15)	67,500	
SE-Common shares		
(90,000 x 5% x $15)		67,500

b)

Common shares (94,500 issued, 300,000 authorized)	$1,147,500
Preferred shares (25,000 issued, 80,000 authorized)	450,000
Retained earnings *	67,500
Total shareholders' equity	$1,665,000

* $220,000 – 62,500 – 22,500 – 67,500 = $67,500

11-23a) 1. A-Cash   750,000
              SE-Common shares   750,000

2. SE-Preferred dividends declared   100,000
    A-Cash   100,000

3. SE-Stock dividends declared   1,360,000
    SE-Stock dividends issuable   1,360,000
    [(750,000 + 50,000) x 10% x $17]

One month after declaration:

    SE-Stock dividends issuable   1,360,000
      SE-Common shares   1,360,000

4. SE-Dividends declared   880,000
    L-Dividends payable   880,000
    [(750,000 + 50,000 + 80,000) x $1.00]

5. SE-Income summary   2,050,000
    SE-Retained earnings   2,050,000

b)

Common shares (880,000 issued and outstanding)	$9,610,000
Preferred shares (50,000 issued and outstanding, 200,000 authorized)	1,000,000
Retained earnings *	5,060,000
Total shareholders' equity	$15,670,000

    * $5,350,000 − 100,000 − 1,360,000 − 880,000 + $2,050,000 = $5,060,000

11-25a) SE-Stock dividends declared   135,000
    SE-Common shares   135,000
    (45,000 x 10% x $30)

b) No entry is needed. The corporation may make a memorandum entry, which is just a notation that the stock split has occurred and the number of shares has been changed. There are now 90,000 shares outstanding.

11-27 a) Ending balance in common shares (in thousands):
$7,500 + (10 x $32) + (5 x $25) = $7,945

   b) Issued during 2004: 10,000 + 5,000
   = 15,000 common shares
   Total issued at end of 2004: 375,000 + 15,000
   = 390,000 common shares

At end of 2003	375,000
Issued in 2004	15,000
Repurchased	(15,000)
Outstanding, end of 2004	375,000

   c) Net income (in thousands)
   $3,750 + net income - $250 - $500   = $4,400
   Net income   = $1,400

11-29 a)

Darby Ltd.
Income Statement
Year Ending December 31, 2003

Revenues		$2,040,000
Cost of Goods Sold		925,700
Gross Margin		1,114,300
Operating expenses:		
Wage expense	$340,800	
Amortization expense	145,000	
Miscellaneous expense	120,900	606,700
Operating income		507,600
Interest expense		42,000
Net Income		$ 465,600

Darby Ltd.
Statement of Retained Earnings
Year Ending December 31, 2003

Retained earnings, January 1	$4,239,500
Net income	465,600
Less:	
Cash dividends declared:	
Preferred shares	
	(167,000)
Common shares	(242,600)
Retained earnings, December 31	$4,295,500

b) Based on the above information, it would appear that Darby Ltd. should be able to continue the dividends on common shares. Net income was $465,600 and the total preferred and common dividends were $409,600. However, the dividend payout ratio for common shares is somewhat high at 81.2% [common dividends $242,600 / (net income $465,600 - preferred dividends $167,000)]. Darby must also generate enough cash to continue to pay dividends. While information on cash flows is not presented, amortization expense of $145,000 was included in the calculation of net income, thereby raising the possibility of $610,600 ($465,600 + $145,000) of cash generated from operations.

In general, a company that pays a constant dividend each year sends a message of stability to shareholders. Thus, it would be helpful to review prior years' common share dividend payments to determine if the $242,600 paid this year is a consistent trend. If so, Darby management would likely try to continue the trend. Also, if net income in 2003 were lower than in prior years, it may be that prior year dividend payout ratios were lower than 81.2%, and that the 81.2% ratio for 2003 is artificially high, caused by a lower than usual net income.

USER PERSPECTIVE SOLUTIONS

11-31 The price/earnings ratio is important because it relates the market price of a share to the actual earnings of a company. This ratio indicates the risk that shareholders bear through investing in common shares, because a high price/earnings ratio means that the market price is based on anticipated earnings rather than actual earnings. If the company does not perform or expand at the expected rate, a correction in the market price occurs. A limitation of the price/earnings ratio is that it can only be compared between companies within the same industry and there may be many reasons why the market may provide a higher valuation of a company's share price, such as higher earnings potential, lower risk with respect to debt repayment, or an assessment of future market share.

11-33 a)

Calculation of dividend received:	
Total expected dividend ($2,000,000 x 40%)	$800,000
Preferred dividends:	
Arrears on Class B (60,000 x $6)	(360,000)
Current year, Class A (20,000 x $10)	(200,000)
Current year, Class B (60,000 x $6)	(360,000)
Available for common shares	0

No dividend could be paid to the common shareholders, as full payment to preferred shareholders would require $920,000.

b) You would expect to receive $24 from your purchase of 100 common shares if the Class B preferred shares are non-cumulative.

Total expected dividend ($2,000,000 x 40%)	$800,000
Preferred dividends:	
Current year, Class A (20,000 x $10)	(200,000)
Current year, Class B (60,000 x $6)	(360,000)
Available for common shares	$240,000
Common shares outstanding	1,000,000
Common dividends per share	$0.24
Common shares to be purchased	x 100
Dividend on 100 common shares	$ 24

11-35 a) If you were to purchase its shares, your prospects of receiving a dividend are slight, because although earnings per share has been increasing more than 15% in recent years, the expenditures in capital assets indicate that the company is growing, and is likely to reinvest its earnings. Your reasoning that the company can declare a $2 or $3 dividend without making a dent in retained earnings overlooks the fact that cash is required to payout the dividend. At the current time, the company can declare a maximum $0.25 dividend before exhausting its current cash balance. In addition, the $50,000 cash on hand is likely required to settle current liabilities as these fall due.

b) During the next five years, your prospects of getting a dividend are much higher because the company is likely to be generating a reasonable return on the capital assets it has purchased, and might no longer need funds for reinvestment and growth. In general, mature companies are more likely to declare dividends than growth companies, because mature companies generate cash that is not required for financing expansion.

c) If Cascade were to enter into such a loan agreement, the prospect of getting a dividend is reduced because the company would be concerned about meeting the debt covenant. Paying out a dividend decreases the assets and equity of Cascade, and increases the risk that long-term debt to equity exceeds 2 to 3. With the additional long-term debt, the long-term debt to equity ratio would be 2.2 to 3 ($4,500,000 / $6,186,000), which already exceeds the 2 to 3 ratio stipulated.

READING AND INTERPRETING PUBLISHED FINANCIAL STATEMENTS SOLUTIONS

11-37 (in millions of US dollars)

    a) 2000 entry:

A-Cash	21	
A-Investment in algroup	3,476	
A-Cash		130
SE-Common shares		3,367

        2001 entry:

A-Cash	60	
A-Investment in algroup	30	
SE-Common shares		90

    b) 2000 entries:

SE-Income summary	618	
SE-Retained earnings		618
SE-Retained earnings	400	
SE-Common shares	130	
A-Cash		530
SE-Dividends declared	155	
L-Dividends payable or A-Cash		155

        2001 entries:

SE-Income summary	5	
SE-Retained earnings		5
SE-Dividends declared	200	
L-Dividends payable of A-Cash		200

c) ROE = $\dfrac{\text{Net income} - \text{Preferred dividends}}{\text{Average common shareholders' equity}}$

2001	2000
ROE = $\dfrac{\$5 - \$8}{(\$8{,}631 + 8{,}867)/2}$	ROE = $\dfrac{\$618 - \$10}{(\$8{,}867 + 5{,}381)/2}$
ROE = 0	ROE = 8.5%

The calculation for 2001 is not meaningful as net income was so low that the preferred dividend declaration marginally reduced the worth of the common shareholders.

d) Note 16 states that Series C and E preferred shares are "eligible for quarterly dividends based on an amount related to the average of the Canadian prime interest rates ...". The prime interest rate may have declined in 2001, resulting in a lower dividend payment.

11-39 a) % reduction in net income:

	2001	2000	1999
	3.05%	1.77%	15.25%

b) The differences in 2000 and 2001 are not significant as they are less than 5% of net income. The 15.25% effect on 1999 net income would be considered significant to most investors.

11-41 a) Multiple Voting Shares entitle the holder to ten votes per share. Subordinate Voting Shares entitle the holder to one vote per share.

b)   **# of votes, June 30, 2001**

Multiple Voting Shares		
(1,224,329 x 10 votes)	12,243,290	68.6%
Subordinate Voting Shares	5,611,000	31.4%
	17,854,290	100%

                              Capital Stock

Multiple Voting Shares	$ 0	0 %
Subordinate Voting Shares	23,412,000	100 %
	$23,412,000	100 %

The Multiple Voting Shares have provided 0% of total capital stock, but hold 68.6% of the votes.

c)   SE-Capital Stock – Subordinate 824,000
          Voting Shares
    SE-Retained Earnings   1,407,000
        A-Cash   2,231,000

d) Repricing of options may occur if the exercise price far exceeds the current market price. If the exercise price is too high, holders will not exercise their options and the options essentially have no value to the holder. If the options were granted as an incentive to employees, this incentive may no longer be effective.

    The repricing of options to a level just above the current market price would restore effectiveness of the option as a mechanism to encourage good employee performance.

    Danier repriced options issued in May 1998 with an original exercise price of $11.25. After repricing, the exercise price was reduced to $6.85, being the average closing market price for the 30 days from and including January 19, 2000.

CHAPTER 12

Financial Statement Analysis

ASSESSING YOUR RECALL SOLUTIONS

12-1 A retrospective analysis is one in which historical data are used to analyze the performance and liquidity of a company. A prospective analysis is one in which data are used to forecast the future (performance and liquidity) of a company.

12-3 The three major types of data that can be used in a time-series or a cross-sectional analysis are:

Raw Data – The raw financial statement data can be used, such as sales revenues, expenses, etc.

Common Size Data – Common size data are obtained by comparing the raw data components to some common denominator. For instance, a common size income statement could be calculated by comparing each line item with the sales revenue for the period. On the balance sheet, the common denominator is usually the total assets.

Ratio Data – Ratios that compare various components of the raw financial statement data can be used as the inputs for these types of analyses.

12-5 The amount of cash produced from operations depends upon several factors. Three of those factors are the accounts receivable, inventory, and accounts payable policies. The leads and lags between the cash outflows for production and the cash inflows from collections on sales are important in understanding the company's cash generating capabilities. The turnover ratios, when converted into the "number of days" form, provide some insight into how long these lags are for a company. Changes in these ratios also provide information about whether there have been significant changes in these policies or in enforcing these policies. The accounts receivable turnover, for instance, tells you how long, on average, it takes to collect an account receivable. Comparing this ratio with a company's stated receivables policy allows you to assess whether or not they are doing a good job of collecting.

12-7 The ROA ratio can be broken down into two ratios: a profit margin ratio and a total asset turnover ratio. The ratios are as follows:

$$ROA = \frac{\text{Net Income} + \text{Interest Expense} \times (1 - \text{Tax Rate})}{\text{Average Total Assets}}$$

$$= \frac{\text{Net Income} + \text{Interest Expense} \times (1 - \text{Tax Rate})}{\text{Sales Revenue}}$$

$$X \qquad \frac{\text{Sales Revenue}}{\text{Average Total Assets}}$$

$$= \text{Profit Margin Ratio} \times \text{Total Asset Turnover}$$

A retail clothing store could employ two different strategies of obtaining a particular ROA. One strategy would be to set prices to achieve a relatively high profit margin. Because of the high prices the total asset turnover might not be as high as it would otherwise be because the company may have to invest more in its stores to attract the kind of clientele that will pay the high prices. The volume of sales per dollar of investment (total asset turnover) may, therefore, be lower. Another store in the same industry may adopt a different strategy in which it charges lower prices (lower profit margin ratio) but makes up for it by not investing as much in its stores and, hopefully, makes up for the lower profit margin with a higher volume per dollar of investment.

12-9 The current ratio is subject to manipulation because at year end the company can adjust its spending and payment patterns to produce a current ratio that is desired. Paying off accounts payable with cash at year end will improve the current ratio, for instance (if original current ratio > 1), but may not be a sign of improved liquidity.

12-11 The earnings per share of a company is calculated by dividing the earnings of the company by the average number of shares that were outstanding during the period. In some companies there exists the possibility that more shares may be issued (other than those currently outstanding) due to agreements such as stock option plans and convertible securities (securities such as convertible debt or convertible preferred shares) that can, at the option of the holder, be converted into common shares. Because of the potential to issue more shares, the calculated earnings per share based on the actual number of shares outstanding may not truly reflect the earnings per share of the company since it may be likely that some investors will exercise their options or convert their debt or preferred shares into common shares. This will have the effect of diluting earnings per share.

The purpose of basic and fully diluted earnings per share is to give the reader of the financial statements some idea of the effect that these conversions might have on the earnings per share number. Basic 'earnings per share' is a reflection of the current earnings and fully diluted earnings per share is a reflection of the worst-case scenario assuming outstanding issuances or conversions occurred.

APPLYING YOUR KNOWLEDGE SOLUTIONS

12-13 a)

	First		Foremost	
Net sales	$300,000	100.0%	$1,440,000	100.0%
Cost of goods sold	(192,000)	(64.0)%	(864,000)	(60.0)%
Operating expenses	(61,200)	(20.4)%	(302,400)	(21.0)%
Interest expense	(3,600)	(1.2)%	(12,000)	(0.83)%
Income tax expense	(13,200)	(4.4)%	(78,000)	(5.42)%
Net income	$30,000	10.0%	$183,600	12.75%

b)

	Total assets	Total shareholders' equity
First – 2004	$522,000	$390,000
– 2003	456,000	312,000
Average	489,000	351,000
Foremost – 2004	$1,800,000	$1,260,000
– 2003	1,680,000	1,170,000
Average	1,740,000	1,215,000

First	Foremost
ROA = $\dfrac{\$30,000+3,600(1-0.3056)}{\$489,000}$	= $\dfrac{\$183,600+12,000(1-0.2982)}{\$1,740,000}$
ROA = 6.6%	= 11.0%
ROE = $30,000/$351,000	= $183,600/$1,215,000
= 8.55%	= 15.11%

c) All performance measures indicate Foremost is more profitable than First. Its profit margin is 2.75% higher, its ROA is 4.4% higher and ROE is 6.56% higher.

d) Two major reasons for Foremost's better performance are its lower cost of goods sold (60% of net sales versus 64%) resulting in higher gross margin percentage of 40%, and a relatively higher asset turnover ratio. Foremost had an asset turnover ratio of 0.83 while First's was only 0.61.

12-15 a) Accounts Receivable Turnover
Campton Electric:
$3,893 / [($542 + $628) / 2] = 6.65
Johnson Electrical:
$1,382 / [($168 + $143) / 2] = 8.89

b) Average number of days required to collect Accounts Receivable:
Campton: 365 / 6.65 = 55 days
Johnson: 365 / 8.89 = 41 days

c) Given that these companies are in the same industry, Johnson would appear to be more efficient in collecting its accounts receivable, as its average collection period is shorter by two weeks.

d) In order to assess management's handling of the collection of accounts receivable, it would be helpful to know the credit terms that each company offers to its customers (i.e. whether customers are asked to pay in 30 days, 45 days, 60 days, etc.). This could then be compared against the turnover in days to determine whether the credit terms are being enforced be helpful.

12-17a)

	Inventory Turnover	Number of days
Year 1:	$463,827 / $65,537 = 7.08	365 / 7.08 = 52 days
Year 2:	$511,125 / $81,560 = 6.27	365 / 6.27 = 58 days
Year 3	$593,350 / $110,338 = 5.38	365 / 5.38 = 68 days
Year 4:	$679,686 / $166,072 = 4.09	365 / 4.09 = 89 days
Year 5:	$708,670 / $225,295 = 3.15	365 / 3.15 = 116 days

b) The inventory turnover has decreased over the five-year period, suggesting a periodic increase in the time that the inventory is held. In fact, the average number of days inventory is held has more than doubled over the five years, to close to four months. This is not favourable. It is possible that this change could be due to a change in the type of inventory that is being sold by the company and, therefore, might not indicate a major problem. Information on such changes is needed in order to comment on the management of inventories.

12-19 a) Current liabilities are $664,892, using the current ratio to calculate the amount:
Current ratio = Current assets / Current liabilities
Current ratio x Current liabilities = Current assets
Current liabilities = Current assets / Current ratio
Current liabilities = $1,462,763 / 2.20 = $664,892

b) Total debt is $2,073,399, using the debt to equity ratio (I) to calculate the amount:
Debt to equity ratio (I) = Total debt / Total assets
Total debt = Debt to equity ratio (I) x Total assets
Total debt = .58 x $3,574,825 = $2,073,399

c) Total equity is $1,501,426 using total assets minus total liabilities ($3,574,825 - $2,073,399).

d) The company has a quick ratio of only 0.89 compared to a current ratio of 2.20. This indicates that the company has a significant amount of inventory or prepaid assets as a current asset on its balance sheet. Financial institutions tend to have larger balances in cash and near cash items, which would tend to result in a higher quick ratio and normally do not carry large balances of inventory. This would appear to rule out classifying the company as a financial institution. It also appears that the company is not a service organization. Service organizations normally do not have large amounts invested in non-current assets. Since only $497,645 of the $1,431,123 increase in total assets is attributable to an increase in current assets, $933,478 has been added to non-current assets during the year. Because of the increase in non-current assets and the large inventory balance, it appears the company is a merchandising or manufacturing company.

e) Net income for the year was $247,530 (1,650,200 shares x $0.15 earnings per share).

f) The company's liquidity is largely dependent upon the nature of the inventory it holds, the speed at which this inventory can be sold, and the cash collected. If the inventory is liquid, then the current ratio of 2.20 indicates that the company is in good shape for the short term. If the inventory is not liquid, then the quick ratio of 0.89 suggests that cash might not be present to extinguish the current liabilities as they fall due.

g) The overall financial position of the company appears to be deteriorating. The quick ratio and earnings per share have declined. The amount of debt relative to assets and equity has increased indicating a larger proportion of debt financing, which increases the risk of the company. A more thorough analysis would be necessary to determine if the company is in serious financial trouble.

h) Significant changes from Year 1 to Year 2 include the discrepancy between the current and quick ratios, the use of debt to finance total assets, the increase in non-current assets, and the decline in earnings per share. The quick ratio declined although the current ratio increased. This indicates that the company has increased its investment in inventory or prepaids, also apparent from the large increase in current assets. The company's use of debt has also increased in Year 2 such that debt is being relied upon to a greater extent than equity, which is not the case in Year 1. This is the result of increased debt financing and possible share redemptions. Non-current assets also increased, and were likely financed through the issuance of additional debt. Finally, earnings per share decreased. While the gross margin on sales did not change significantly, the increased debt burden undoubtedly had a major impact, resulting in a reduction in net income and earnings per share.

12-21 a) Return on Shareholders' Equity:

ROE
Year 1: $1,583 / $24,664 = 6.4%
Year 2: $3,830 / $32,415 = 11.8%
Year 3: $6,755 / $51,515 = 13.1%

b) Return on assets:

	Profit Margin Ratio	Total Asset Turnover	ROA
Year 1:	[$1,583 + $896(0.75)] / $42,798 = 5.3%	$42,798 / $48,744 = 0.88	4.7%
Year 2:	[$3,830 + $1,441(0.7)] / $54,060 = 9.0%	$54,060 / $65,258 = 0.83	7.5%
Year 3:	[$6,755 + $2,112(0.7)] / $76,023 = 10.8%	$76,023 / $98,654 = 0.77	8.3%

c) ROA and ROE have been positive and increasing over the three-year period. This would indicate improved performance over time. The actual performance depends upon what other companies in the same industry have been able to do in the same time period. The improvement has come from improved profit margins as evidenced from the change in the profit margin ratio and the slightly declining asset turnover. The company is also effectively applying leverage since the ROE exceeds the ROA.

12-23 a)

	D/E (I)	D/E (II)	D/E(III)
Year 1:	$1,025 / $2,325 = 44%	$1,025 / $1,300 = 79%	$600 / $1,900 = 32%
Year 2:	$1,525 / $3,325= 46%	$1,525 / $1,800 = 85%	$1,000 / $2,800 = 36%
Year 3:	$2,150 / $4,350 = 49%	$2,150 / $2,200 = 98%	$1,400 / $3,600 = 39%

	Times Interest Earned
Year 1:	$500 / $60 = 8.3
Year 2:	$800 / $100 = 8.0
Year 3:	$1,000 / $135 = 7.4

b) All three debt/equity ratios show worsening trends over the three years. There would be some concern if this trend continues and if it accelerates. The times interest earned ratio indicates that the company is currently earning a sufficient amount of income to meet its interest obligations, although this trend is steadily worsening which may also be a concern.

12-25

Trans-action	a) Current Ratio	b) Quick Ratio	c) A/R Turnover	d) Inventory Turnover	e) D/E(I)	f) ROA	g) ROE
1	+	+	-	+	-	+	+
2	NE	NE	+	NE	NE	NE	NE
3	*	-	NE	-	+	-	NE
4	+	+	NE	NE	+	-	NE
5	-	-	NE	NE	+	-	-
6	NE	NE	NE	NE	NE	NE	NE
7	+	+	NE	NE	-	-	-

*The ratio will be affected, but the direction of the effect cannot be determined from the information given. Since the same amount will be added or subtracted from the numerator as well as the denominator, the change in the ratio will depend on whether the ratio was greater or less than 1.0 to begin with.

12-27a) Net income for 2002 = $0.76 per share x 28,500 shares
= $21,660

b) Earnings per share for 2003 = $24,510 / 28,500
= $0.86 per share

c) Earnings per share figures are usually included in the annual report on the face of the income statement for each year reported. They are usually reported just below net income. They could also be reported in the notes to the financial statements, although very few companies will report earnings per share in this manner.

d) If Signal decides to split its common shares 2 for 1, then the earnings per share must also be split in two because the same net income must be spread out over twice as many shares. The 2004 earnings per share amount is also affected, because the comparative income statement must present both earnings per share figures as though the split had occurred in 2004. This retroactive treatment is provided so that comparability is maintained.

12-29 a) Ratios for A-Tec and B-Sci:

		A-Tec		Bi-Sci	
		2003	2002	2003	2002
(1)	Current ratios	1.16	.95	2.25	2.17
(2)	Working capital	$11	($2)	$30	$28
(3)	Rec. turnover	31.7 times	45 times	30.5 times	30 times
(4)	Inv. Turnover	15.6 times	22.5 times	15.2 times	15 times
(5)	Asset turnover	2.8 times	3.2 times	3.6 times	3.8 times

(6) Total debt to

total assets	82.0%	81.7%	14.2%	15.4%

(7) Sh. Equity to

total assets	18.0%	18.3%	85.8%	84.6%
(8) Gross margin ratio	34.2%	33%	25.4%	25%
(9) Return on sales	10%	11.9%	9.8%	9.2%
(10) Return on assets	28.1%	38.5%	35.5%	35.3%
(11) Return on equity	155.7%	210.5%	41.4%	41.7%

Supporting calculations:

A-Tec:	2003	2002
(1) Current ratio (current assets/current liabilities)	78/67	38/40
(2) Working capital (current assets – current Liabilities)	78/67	38/40
(3) Acc. receivables turnover (sales/net acc. rec.)	950/30	675/15
(4) Inventory turnover (cost of goods sold/inv.)	625/40	450/20
(5) Asset turnover (sales/total assets)	950/338	675/208
(6) Total debt to total assets (total liab./total assets)	277/338	170/208
(7) Sh. equity to total assets (Sh. equity/total assets)	61/338	38/208
(8) Gross margin ratio [(sales – cost of goods sold) /sales]	(950-625) /950	(675-450) /675
(9) Return on sales (net income/sales)	95/950	80/675
(10) Return on assets (net income/total assets)	95/338	80/208

(11)   Return on equity (net income/Sh. Equity)   95/61   80/38

Bi-Sci:	2003	2002
(1) Current ratio (current assets/current liabilities)	54/24	52/24
(2) Working capital (current assets – current Liabilities)	54-24	52-24
(3) Acc. receivables turnover (sales/net acc. rec.)	610/20	600/20
(4) Inventory turnover (cost of goods sold/inv.)	455/30	450/30
(5) Asset turnover (sales/total assets)	610/169	600/156
(6) Total debt to total assets (total liab./total assets)	24/169	24/156
(7) Sh. equity to total assets (Sh. equity/total assets)	145/169	132/156
(8) Gross margin ratio [(sales – cost of goods sold) /sales]	(610-455) /610	(600-450) /600
(9) Return on sales (net income/sales)	60/610	55/600
(10) Return on assets (net income/total assets)	60/169	55/156
(11) Return on equity (net income/Sh. Equity)	60/145	55/132

b) The following analysis is separated into liquidity, solvency, leverage and profitability analysis.

Liquidity: Bi-Sci appears to be in a better liquidity position. Its current ratio is much higher than A-Tec's and its working capital is also higher. A-Tec's current ratio and working capital have improved but they are still lower. The accounts receivable turnover and inventory turnover also measure liquidity because they measure the amount of time before these items will be converted to cash in the operating cycle. Both of these ratios remained constant for Bi-Sci in 2003. A-Tec's ratios declined in 2003 and are now closer to Bi-Sci's. It may be that A-Tec's ratios in 2002 were unusually high and are now closer to those of other companies.

Solvency: Bi-Sci is in a much better solvency position as measured by the total debt to total assets and total shareholders' equity to total assets ratios. Bi-Sci is financed mostly by shares while A-Tec is financed mostly by borrowing.

Leverage: A-Tec is using much more leverage than Bi-Sci. Since A-Tec is financed mostly by debt, its return on equity (net income/shareholders' equity) will be much higher when the rate of earnings exceeds the interest rate on the debt. Leverage is best measured by comparing the return on assets to the return on equity. With high leverage, and a return on assets in excess of interest rates, the return on equity for a company like A-Tec will be very high. The returns of the two companies are calculated as follows:

	A-Tec		Bi-Sci	
	2003	2002	2003	2002
Return on assets	28.1%	38.5%	35.5%	35.3
Return on equity	155.7%	210.5%	41.4%	41.7%

Profitability: The companies are very similar in profitability measures. The return on sales is about the same both years for Bi-Sci, but has declined for A-Tec. Similarly, Bi-

Sci's ROA is the same for both years while A-Tec has declined by 27% of the 2002 levels. Thus, overall, Bi-Sci has maintained profitability while A-Tec has fallen off. However, A-Tec increased its sales by 40% in 2003 to go along with the expansion in assets and Bi-Sci had no growth in 2003. Also, A-Tec has high gross margin ratio in both years.

Determining which company is the better investment for a shareholder depends on the amount of risk the shareholder is willing to absorb. The return on equity for A-Tec is very high. As long as the return on assets stays high, there will be a good return to shareholders. An important question is will the growth in sales continue. On the other hand, the high leverage makes A-Tec much more risky for shareholders. Bi-Sci appears to be a much better credit risk from a lender's standpoint. It has a much better liquidity and solvency position, less leverage, and less risk that debts will not be paid.

12-31 From 2 and 3, accounts receivable turnover

$$= \frac{\$23,650,000}{(\$2,042,500 + 2003\ A/R)/2} = 11.0$$

Then, $2,042,500 + 2003 A/R = ($23,650,000 x 2) / 11.0
          2003 A/R   = $2,257,500

Then, Let A = Net income + Interest expense x (1 – tax rate)
          B = 2003 Inventory
          C = 2003 Current liabilities
          D = Cost of goods sold expense

From 6. Profit margin ratio = 12.5% = A / $23,650,000   (a)

From 5. Return on assets = 20% = A /[$15,050,000 +967,600
                                    + 2,257,500 + B +
                                    8,933,000]/2   (b)

From 4. Inventory turnover = 5.1 = D / [($3,698,000 + B)]/2 (c)

From 1.   Current ratio=2.5=($967,500 + 2,257,500 + B) / C (d)

Then, from (a),   A = $2,956,250

And, from (b),   A = 20% x ($27,208,000 + B) / 2
                         B = $2,354,500

And, from (c),   5.1 = D / [($3,698,000 + 2,354,500)]/2
                         D = $15,433,875

And, from (d),   2.5 = ($967,500 + 2,257,500 +
                                    2,354,500) / C
                         C = $2,231,800

Now, Let E = tax rate
     F = Interest expense
     G = Net income

Then, A = G + F x (1 – E) = $2,956,250   (e)

     Income before taxes x tax rate = Income tax expense
     [$4,636,375 – F] x E = $1,204,000   (f)

     Income from operations – interest expense – income tax
                         expense = net income
     $4,636,375 – F - $1,204,000 = G   (g)

Then, substituting (g) into (e):
     $4,636,375 – F - $1,204,000 + F x (1 – E) = $2,956,250
     $476,125 = F – F x (1 – E) = F – F + F x E = F x E

And, substituting this into (f):
     $\frac{\$476,125}{F}$ x ($4,636,375 – F) = $1,204,000
     $476,125 x ($4,636,375 – F) = $1,204,000 x F
     $476,125 x $4,636,375 = $1,680,125 x F
     F = $1,313,887

Then, E = $1,204,000 / ($4,636,375 – 1,313,887)
        = 36.24%

And, $G = \$4,636,375 - 1,313,887 - 1,204,000$
$= \$2,118,488$

USER PERSPECTIVE PROBLEMS

12-33 Perhaps the easiest way to influence the ratio is to try to increase net income. A change in the revenue recognition method to recognize revenue earlier in the company's cash-to-cash cycle could have this impact. Accelerating the recognition of revenue under existing methods could also cause an increase in net income. Companies might speed up shipments of goods, for instance, if revenues are recognized at the time of shipment. Management could also decide to delay the acquisition of new capital assets. When new assets replace old ones, total assets usually increases, which lowers the ROA.

12-35 From the perspective of an auditor, the following ratios might be helpful in identifying abnormalities:

- ROA: This ratio reflects the rate of return that a company earns on all assets. If this ratio is significantly different from that of other companies in the same industry, abnormalities or fraud might exist. This ratio should be examined through its component parts—the profit margin ratio and the asset turnover.

- Accounts receivable turnover: This ratio indicates the speed at which receivables are collected. If the company has created fictitious sales, then turnover would be much lower than expected because the accounts receivable associated with the fake sales are not collected. This can alert the auditor to fraud.

- Accounts payable turnover: This ratio reflects the speed at which payables are paid. If the company is creating fictitious sales, then this ratio would be much higher than expected because the cost of goods sold associated with the fake sales does not correspond to a portion of accounts payable.

   In general, auditors use both time-series analysis and cross-sectional analysis to alert them to irregularities or fraud. Auditors focus on areas where significant changes occurred from the prior year and on those areas that differ materially from industry averages.

12-37 Ratios that would help the decision-maker in arriving at a decision or to identify areas for further analysis include:
- Decrease in net income from a/an:
    1. Decrease in sales or an increase in cost of sales:
        Gross Profit Margin
    2. Increase in total operating expenses:
        Gross Profit Margin and Return on Sales
        Horizontal and Vertical Analysis
    3. Increase in an individual operating expense:
        Horizontal and Vertical Analysis

- Sufficient cash to make debt payments:
    Current Ratio
    Quick Ratio

- Long-term debt higher than the industry as a whole:
    Debt to Equity
    Long-term Debt to Assets

- Effective utilization of assets:
    Asset Turnover Ratio
    Return on Assets

- Comparison of profitability in relation to invested capital:
    Return on Equity

- Whether the decline in economic activity affected accounts receivable collections:
    Accounts Receivable Turnover

- Whether the company was successful in reducing inventory investment:
    Inventory Turnover

- Determining which company provides more earnings per share:

  Earnings Per Share

  Price/earnings Ratio

READING AND INTERPRETING PUBLISHED FINANCIAL STATEMENTS SOLUTIONS

12-39 a) (in thousands of US dollars)

Inventory turnover = $\dfrac{\text{Cost of goods sold}}{\text{Average inventory}}$

= $\dfrac{\$25,927}{(\$799 + 3,117))/2}$

= 13.24 times

Accounts receivable turnover = $\dfrac{\text{Sales}}{\text{Average accounts receivable}}$

= $\dfrac{\$134,320}{(\$18,689 + 28,620)/2}$

= 5.68 times

b)

	2001	2000
1. Current ratio	$144,906 / $59,109 = 2.45	$162,605 / $55,943 = 2.91
2. Quick ratio	$142,328 / $59,109 = 2.41	$157,959 / $55,943 = 2.82
3. D/E (I)	$64,076/ $235,699 = 27.2%	$55,943 / $218,587 = 25.6%
4. D/E (III)	$4,967 / $176,590 = 2.8%	$ 0 / $162,644 = 0 %

c)

Balance Sheets

	2001	2000
ASSETS:		
Current assets:		
Cash	18.8	58.8
Short-term investments	33.1	0.0
Accounts receivable	8.5	13.5
Inventory	0.3	1.4
Other	0.8	0.7
Total current assets	61.5	74.4
Capital assets	18.3	19.4
Goodwill	15.9	0.0
Other	4.3	6.2

Total assets	100.0	100.0

LIABILITIES & SHAREHOLDERS'
EQUITY:

Current liabilities	25.1	25.6
Long-term liabilities	2.1	0.0
Total liabilities	27.2	25.6
Shareholders' equity:		
Share capital	164.7	170.1
Contributed surplus	2.1	2.3
Retained earnings (deficit)	(94.0)	(98.0)
Total shareholders' equity	72.8	74.4
Total liabilities and share-holders' equity	100.0	100.0

Income Statements

	2001	2000
Sales	100.0	100.0
Cost of sales	19.3	29.9
	80.7	70.1
Expenses:		
Advertising	16.4	21.1
Selling, general, and administrative	46.0	54.4
Research and development	18.8	27.9
Other	4.1	7.4
(Gain)/loss on investments	1.8	(9.3)
Interest (income) expense	(4.0)	0.8
Income tax expense	3.0	3.0
	(5.4)	(35.2)

The balance sheet shows a 12.9% reduction in current assets comprised of a 6.9% reduction in very liquid assets and 5% reduction in accounts receivable. The goodwill on the 2000 balance sheet was written off in 2001. The company has almost no long-term debt, and overall liabilities have held constant, providing about one quarter of the company's asset financing. The company's retained earnings deficit is very large, being almost equal to the total asset base in both years.

On the income statement, cost of sales dropped from 29.9% in 2000, to 19.3% in 2001. Almost all expense categories were reduced in 2001 (as a % of sales) with the largest cost savings being for research and development, a drop of 9.1% and selling, general, and administrative, a drop of 8.4%. The decline in costs in 2001 reduced the year's loss to only 5.4% of sales, a significant improvement over the 35.2% of sales deficit in 2000.

d) The company reported a positive cash flow from operating activities in 2001 of $15,144, a significant improvement over the 2000 negative cash flow of $30,015. The only financing activity in 2001 was $10,000 spent to retire Novell obligations. In 2000 the company had raised $149,735 from issuance of common and preferred shares. There was minimal activity in investing cash flows in 2000, but in 2001, $78,076 was invested in short-term investments and $16,338 of cash restricted for participation rights obligations.

In summary, the company issued a significant amount of equity in the prior year. This, along with improved operations in 2001, generated cash for short-term investments.

e) The company's short-term liquidity appears sound with respectable current and quick ratios, and ample cash reserves on the balance sheet. The debt/equity ratios are very low and there is no long-term bank debt. Thus, the balance sheet appears very strong, although the virtual absence of inventory is worrying. Although a high tech company may not have a warehouse full of inventory in the traditional sense, inventory levels have dropped 74% from the prior year.

The income statement provides a different story. The company reported a large loss in 2000, a smaller loss in 2001, and the overall deficit is approximately the same size as the company's asset base. Thus, profitability is an issue, although the reduced loss in 2001 may be an indication that the 2000 infusion of capital has allowed the company to restructure its operations and get its costs under control.

The 2001 positive cash flow from operations may confirm this.

Any investment in Corel would definitely need to be based on future expectations, and not the company's past year results.

f) This could be due to temporary differences in the year. For example, in the year with a net loss, actual warranty costs claimed on the tax return may be greater than the estimated warranty expense. This difference will create a future income tax liability on the balance sheet, resulting in income tax expense.

12-41 a) (all amounts in thousands)

ROE = $\dfrac{\text{Net Income - Preferred Dividends}}{\text{Average shareholders' equity}}$

= $\dfrac{\$(7,006)}{(\$68,523 + 56,126)/2}$

= 11.2%

Accounts receivable turnover = $\dfrac{\text{Sales}}{\text{Average accounts receivable}}$

= $\dfrac{\$81,640}{(\$23,112 + 9,486)/2}$

= 5.01

b)

	2000	2001
1. Current ratio	$50,067 / $12,604 = 3.97	$50,648 / $15,090 = 3.36
2. Quick ratio	$44,214 / $12,604 = 3.51	$42,429 / $15,090 = 2.81
3. D/E (I)	$18,157 / $74,283 = 24.4%	$20,480 / $89,003 = 23%
4. D/E (II)	$18,157 / $56,126 = 32.3%	$20,480 / $68,523 = 29.9%

c)

Balance Sheets

	2000	2001
ASSETS:		
Current assets:		
Cash	8.1	6.5
Short-term marketable securities	33.8	15.1
Accounts receivable	12.8	26.1
Income tax receivable	2.3	0.0
Revenue receivable in excess of amount billed	2.5	0.0
Inventory	6.3	6.9
Prepaid expenses	1.6	2.3
Total current assets	67.4	56.9
Capital assets	24.4	25.8
Long-term investments	2.0	7.8
Future income tax recoverable	6.2	9.5
Total assets	100.0	100.0

LIABILITIES & SHAREHOLDERS'
EQUITY:

Accounts payable	14.6	15.6
Other	2.2	1.3
Mortgage payable	7.7	6.1
Total liabilities	24.5	23.0
Shareholders' equity:		
Share capital	51.9	49.4
Retained earnings (deficit)	23.6	27.6
Total shareholders' equity	75.5	77.0
Total liabilities and share-holders' equity	100.0	100.0

Income Statements

	2000	2001
Revenues	100.0	100.0
Expenses:		
Labour and materials	18.8	17.0
Research and development	38.4	37.9
Selling and marketing	24.6	22.0
General and administration and other	14.6	10.2
Restructuring	(0.4)	0.0
Income tax expense	1.9	4.5
	0.4	8.4

On the balance sheet, the liquid assets have shifted to accounts receivable from cash and short-term marketable securities. Accounts receivable increased 144% and liquid assets decreased by 62% of total assets. The company reported a larger profit in 2001, which meant that retained earnings in the shareholders' equity section of the balance sheet increased by 40% in 2001. Revenues increased by 74%, while operating expenses increased by only 60%. R&D costs representing 44% of the 2001 operating expenses were up by 70%.

d) Both years' cash flows show inflows from the issue of shares, although $5.4 million in shares issued was reduced by $12 million in 2000.

   $5.4 million in share issues and $11.6 million net redemption of marketable securities was utilized to acquire $12 million in capital assets and $5.4 million in other long-term investments.

   The cash from operations declined dramatically to $319,000 in 2001 from $7 million in 2000 driven by a $10 million drop in working capital.

e) Mosaid uses very little leverage, as evidenced by the low D/E (I) ratio of 24.5% in 2000, which fell to 23% in 2001. Note that Mosaid does not need debt as it has substantial cash and short-term marketable securities.

f) Earnings per share will likely decrease, at least initially, as the net income is allocated over a larger number of common shares outstanding. Earnings per share may later recover if the company uses the additional $5.4 million of cash to invest and thus increase net income proportionately.

12-43 Answers to this question will depend on the company selected.

BEYOND THE BOOK SOLUTION